In Search of
Authenticity of
Self and English

良質なテキストで自己成熟 ＆ 英語成熟をめざして

JN102654

Masao KANAOKA
Judy YONEOKA

EIHŌSHA

ACKNOWLEDGMENTS

The editors and publisher acknowledge permission to reproduce
the following copyright writing in this book:

Unit 9 *Moral Limits of Market Society and Importance of
Practical Wisdom*
Used by permission of Macmillan Publishers.

Unit 11 *Teaching and Learning* Wisdom—
Ultimate Goal of Higher Education
Used by permission of Taylor & Francis Group.

PRINTED IN JAPAN

はじめに

本書の目的と特徴

　大学生となったみなさんは、今、どこに向かっていますか。大学の中で、あるいは授業を通して英語とどのように向き合っているでしょうか。大学生活を楽しみたい一方で、これまでとあまり変わらない「生き方と英語の捉え方」を、続けてはいないでしょうか。そうした人生観と英語観を見つめ直し、両者を大きな視点から構築してもらうために本書はつくられました。「自分というにんげんの確かな成長（自己成熟）とそれを支えていく英語学習の成長（英語成熟）」を実現していくことが、本書の目的です。

　この 2 つの成熟（自己成熟＆英語成熟）をめざして用意されたコンテクス（学習の流れ）は、極めて<u>正統性（ほんもの指向）</u>を意識したものです。そこには以下の大きな問いが投げ込まれています。

● 　世界のトップレベルの大学が考えている、本当の意味での「大学生力」とは何なのか？
● 　何が本当の意味での「人生の成功」と言えるのか？
● 　科目履修（単位取得）と成績の優劣をこえ、何を「真の学修成果」として身につけておくべきなのか？
● 　これらの観点に立った時、確立すべき「英語（学習）観」はどのようなものになるべきなのか？
● 　今を生きる偉人、そして過去に生き、心を揺さぶる遺訓を残した賢人たちから何を学び取るべきなのか？
● 　これまでの自分（という一人の人間）には、どのような視点や信念や価値観が欠けていたのか？
● 　自分を見つめ直し、励まし、育てていくうえで、英語をどのように自己体内化していけばよいのか？

　このような難題と冷静に向き合い、確かな答えを出していく─そこに本書はウェイトを置いています。

本書の構成と学習ステップ

　考えを深め、そこに英語をなじませ、自分の分身にしながら着実に自己成長を進めていく─これに向けて 6 つのステージと 15 の Unit が用意されています（目次と補足のビジュアルを参照）。

Authenticity Stage 1 (Units 1-2) / 大学入学試験（求める能力と人間像）について─米国と英国の有名大学からの事例（目的と試験内容について）

Authenticity Stage 2 (Units 3-4) / グローバル社会を生きるうえで、必要不可欠となる英語モチベーション（動機づけ）について─新たな視点（学習理論）と著名な研究者の考え

Authenticity Stage 3 (Units 5-7) / 大学教育の目的と理念について─卒業までに身につけたい大学生力と人間構築力の中味

Authenticity Stage 4 (Units 8-11) / 大学生活を終え、市民や社会人となり、世の中に参画していくうえで重要となるテーマについて─政治（学）の役割と目指すべき人間社会の姿

Authenticity Stage 5 (Units 12-14) / 幕末〜明治の時代を中心に活躍した、偉大なる 3 名の日本人からの教えについて―欧米世界からみた文明の真の意味、そして目指すべき人間像と英語を学び、使う目的

Authenticity Stage 6 (Unit 15) / 大学教育、英語学習、社会観、世界観、歴史観などをふまえ、もつべき人生哲学と実践すべき英語学習について―確かな自己成長と成熟した英語観の証明に向けて

まとめとして、「ほんものに出会う」、「本質を見抜いていく」、「ぶれない自分をつくっていく」。このために 6 つのステージが敷かれています。

　　各 Unit の中身も系統立てています。具体的には *1. Precept*：本文（パッセージ）に関連した英文と和訳の提示（= Unit 全体のポイント理解に向けたヒント）、*2. Prudence and Insight*：本文に入る前の思考活動（日本語によるペアワークやグループワーク）、*3. Understanding the Gist of Each Paragraph of the Main Passage*：本文の各パラグラフの重要ポイントの解説、*4. Main Passage and Oral Reading*：本文の内容理解と音読練習、*5. Vocabulary Building ― Important Words / Phrases / Sentences*：内容理解に向けた語彙力の獲得と増強、*6. Responsive Writing: In Pursuit of Wider Views and Deeper Thoughts*：理解した内容に対する自分の考えや意見、新たな視点の提示（ライティング）、*7. Note Taking and Exchanging Ideas―Listening Practice and Follow-Up Discussion*：そうした発信活動を使った協同活動（ペア・グループワーク）をもとに、さらなる発見や気づきへの探求（リスニング＆ノートテイキング）、*8. Reflection with a Pure Mind ― 素心深考*：この Unit で経験した学習活動の振り返り。このターム（素心深考）を世に広めたのは、数学者の広中平祐氏です（数学のノーベル賞といわれるフィールズ賞を受賞。ハーバード大学で博士号を取得。元山口大学学長。故人）。「素朴な心に立ち返り、じっくりと考えてみる」―こうした思い（重要性）が込められいます。

　　自身の「英語力」を鍛え、高めていくことは大切です。それと同時に「英語という存在」（外国語、1 つの言語、母語とは違った存在、自己成長を助けてくれる確かな媒体 etc.）について、じっくりと考え、向き合いながら自分が納得できる答えを見つけ出してください。成熟した大学生、そして豊かな内面世界を携えた魅力的な人となっていくために―。

　　本書刊行にあたり、この英語テキストに込められたこだわり（理念や願い、正統的な英語教育と学習の道しるべ、伝統とそこに息づく価値体系を重んじる大学文化の普遍性）を真摯に理解し、深い共感を示してくださった英宝社の方々に深く御礼申し上げます。

著者

Contents

Visual Diagram of Contents

Combination of Authentic Self-Growth & Convincing English Language Skills

Key Aspects   ### Learning Themes

* True Meaning of Campus Life

* True Aim of Learning
  and Using English

> **Authenticity Stage 6: Unit 15**
> Learning and Using English in College—Refinement of Its *Raison D'être*

* Japanese Civilization

* A Mature Human Society

* English Language Education

> **Authenticity Stage 5: Units 12-14**
> Japan's Historic Challenge—Establishing Values Comparable to the Western Standard

* Public Philosophy

* Practical Wisdom

* Good Human Society

> **Authenticity Stage 4: Units 8-11**
> Essential Discussion Themes on Campus and in the Classroom

* Social Viewpoint

* Core Part of Self

* Life Philosophy

> **Authenticity Stage 3: Units 5-7**
> Sacred Goal and Mission of College Education

* Globalization

* Identity Development

> **Authenticity Stage 2: Units 3-4**
> Motivation to Learn English as a Foreign Language

* Maturity of Inner Part of Self

* Good Character

> **Authenticity Stage 1: Units 1-2**
> College Entrance Examinations

Unit 1

College Entrance Examinations in the United States
The Purpose of Written Statements Focusing on "Who I am"

1 —Precept—

Character formation has traditionally been considered crucial in U.S. higher education. When applying for prominent Ivy League schools, writing which emphasizes "who I really am" plays an important role.

米国の大学教育では、人格形成は伝統的に重んじられている。有名なアイビーリーグ校へ出願する場合、「自分はまさにこういうにんげんなのです」と訴えた英語ライティングが大きなカギを握ることになる。

2 —Prudence and Insight—

米国の大学入試では、日本の「大学入学共通テスト」のようなマークシートの試験 SAT があります。これとは別に〈重視されている試験〉があります(例.コロンビア大学、プリンストン大学、ダートマスカレッジといった Ivy League の有名大学)。それはどのような試験か、その内容と目的について話し合ってください。

ヒント(キーワード):自身にふれたライティング、自己アイデンティティ、成熟した内面世界、地域と社会への関心と取り組み

1

Study Focus: College Admission Policy and Required Written Statements in U.S.

Gist of Each Paragraph

Introduction

[P1] Requirement of personal statement in addition to SAT.

[P2] Duties of admitted students (i.e., new college students): (1) to be a more mature person, (2) to gain sufficient academic knowledge and learning skills.

Body

[P3] Writing Test—Case 1: Columbia University. Focus on (1) personal values, (2) how to contribute to Columbia's diverse and collaborative community.

[P4] Writing Test—Case 2: Princeton University. Focus on (1) concrete experience of facing a difficult situation and generating an appropriate solution.

[P5] Writing Test—Case 3: Dartmouth College. Focus on (1) personal experience of a civic engagement or contribution to a given community or society.

Conclusion

[P6] Common direction of Ivy League Schools = selecting *the right person* with extensive academic knowledge, experience of civic engagement for social contribution, and insight and passion for solving difficult problems and issues.

4 —Main Passage and Oral Reading—

[P1] In addition to the U.S. nationwide standardized entrance examination called *SAT¹*, personal statements are traditionally required for admission to U.S. colleges and universities. Whether taking the form of a formal essay or short statements, the writing plays an important part of the college application procedure. The aim is to find *promising* candidates—who must be competitive, spontaneous, highly motivated, self-responsible, self-controlled, etc. In sum, *being mature* is requisite for college enrollment.

[P2] Why? This is because a foremost duty of college students is to be capable and responsible in order to lead a meaningful and challenging campus life. They are encouraged to become mature. To this end, while gaining wider academic knowledge and hands-on skills, the achievement of a matured self is deemed crucial. The following paragraphs describe the information for required written statements at US Ivy League Universities.

[P3] Every year, Columbia University produces what they term "Columbia-specific questions" as the writing supplement to their entrance examination process. They aim to identify "intellectual curiosity, habits of mind, love of learning and sense of self". The example questions on their website range from making simple lists of books and other literature enjoyed in high school to a detailed description of "your own perspective, viewpoint or lived experience" and how it can positively contribute to the diversity of the Columbia academic community. Another question asks the potential candidate to succinctly describe "something that brings you joy". Through these and similar writing prompts, the Columbia-specific questions demonstrate with clarity not only the qualities desired of a potential student, but also define and reflect the ideal Columbia University experience itself.

[P4] Similarly, Princeton University requires a writing supplement which includes an academic-oriented prompt based on the prospective student's desired degree, in addition to a graded sample of previous student writing. Three other writing questions are carefully tailored to allow those in charge of selection to carefully understand and critically review the overall life experience, analytical abilities and emotional maturity of the applicant. Examples include discussions of meaningful past activities or experiences, future applications of insights gained from discussion about a difficult issue, and, as at Colombia, "What brings you joy?". An especially unique example question is "What song represents the soundtrack of your life at this moment?" These questions give applicants a chance to make their voices heard and demonstrate their personal values, skills of evaluation and application, and creativity.

[P5] In its supplementary writing section, the entrance examination of

Dartmouth College requires its students to write four essays in total, one of which is a personal statement. The other three supplementary short writings include a self-introduction, reasons for wanting to enter Dartmouth, and a final short essay in response to a choice of prompts. Topics for the latter include "What excites you?", "In what ways do you hope to make—or are you making—an impact?" and "What do you wonder and think about?". Within the prompts, quotes are included by influential individuals who reflect the Dartmouth educational policy such as civil rights activist *Dolores Huerta²*.

[P6] With such questions, U.S. top-notch institutions are eager to find attractive candidates. Although individual writing prompts may differ, they all point to *a common direction*. That is, the goal of admission process lies in securing the *right* candidate, i.e., one with extensive academic views, enriched insights in the face of hard-to-resolve life situations, and solid passion and spirit for challenging and solving difficult issues and questions. Also, the prospective student should demonstrate the ability to work together in an analytical, objective, and creative manner leading to new ideas and solutions, as this competence plays an integral role in the university academic community.

[602 words]

語 注

SAT¹　大学進学適性試験（米国の大学進学希望者を対象にした共通試験）

Dolores Huerta²　ドロレス・フエルタ（1932-）。ニューメキシコ州生まれの米国女性運動家。移民や女性、さらには労働者の人権問題をめぐって議論を戦わせ、その主張と行動、そして言動は注目を浴びている。

■ Checking Your Oral Reading Speed *Words Per Minute (WPM)*
{Self / Pair / Group}

Measure your WPM using your cellphone or other timing device. Read the passage aloud and determine whether your speed is *sufficient* for reading texts by using the WPM index below.

Words Per Minute (WPM) Index

Total Words ÷ Your Reading Time (in seconds) × 60 = Your WPM

◆ Target WPM = 110 – 125. vs. * *My WPM* = (   )

If your WPM is in the range of the Target WPM, your reading-aloud speed is sufficient to read texts. If your WPM is beyond 125, it is nearing native WPM. If your WPM is below 100, you need to work on your reading speed.

5 —Vocabulary Building—
Important Words / Phrases / Sentences

This vocabulary list contains important words, phrases and sentences from the passage. Using an English-Japanese dictionary or website, please write the Japanese meaning in blank parts.

English	Japanese
[P1]	
personal statements	自己説明
admission to U.S. colleges and universities	
plays an important part of	
promising candidates	有望な候補者
competitive, spontaneous, highly motivated, self-responsible, self-controlled	
requisite for	... （へ）の要件
[P2]	
a foremost duty	最重要課題
meaningful and challenging	有意義でやりがいのある
the achievement of a matured self	成熟した人間となる

the information for required written statements	必須となるライティング説明文の情報
[P3]	
as the writing supplement to	
intellectual curiosity, habits of mind, love of learning and sense of self	知的好奇心、思考の習慣化、学習意欲と自分らしさ
the potential candidate	
succinctly describe	手際よく説明する
through these and similar writing prompts	こうしたものと同様のライティングテーマを通して
the qualities desired of a potential student	有能視される学生（受験生）に求められる資質
[P4]	
an academic-oriented prompt	学業面を中心にしたテーマ
a graded sample of previous student writing	成績がついた、これまでのライティングサンプル
are carefully tailored	入念につくられている
those in charge of selection	選考担当者
analytical abilities and emotional maturity	
future applications of insights	将来に応用していける洞察力
make their voices heard	自分の声（考え）を聞いてもらう
skills of evaluation and application	
[P5]	
in response to a choice of prompts	選んだテーマへの答えとして
civil rights activist	市民権運動の活動家
[P6]	
top-notch institutions	
in the face of hard-to-resolve life situations	解決が難しい人生の状況に出会う
in an analytical, objective, and creative manner	
plays an integral role in	
the university academic community	大学という学びの共同体

<Total: 31 Useful Expressions>

6 —Responsive Writing: In Pursuit of Wider Views and Deeper Thoughts—

From the passage, what point(s) have you gained or learned as good hints for making yourself a *prudent and insightful* person? This *Eureka* (new finding) will become a *good medium* for generating a big question or obtaining new knowledge and findings through discussion with your classmates. Describe your *Eureka* in 100-120 words.

My *Eureka* (New Finding) from the Passage   (   ) words

7 —Note Taking and Exchanging Ideas—Listening Practice and Follow-Up Discussion—

Write down keywords, phrases, or important points from your classmates' presentations on *My Eureka*. Then hold a discussion using this information. Try to raise a big question or obtain further new knowledge through active interaction.

8 —Reflection with a Pure Mind—
素心深考 ＊Unit 1 からの学び

　英語を１つの外国語として学んできたのか？それとも教科の１つとして学んできたのか？　いずれにせよ、じつはよく考えたことがこなかった…。そうであるなら、そこには盲点があります。それはおそらく、米国人などの母語話者が自国の大学入試を受験するにあたり、「英語を使って示すべき能力とはいったい何か？」という問いに対する答えでもあります。何が入試問題を通して真剣に問われ、験（ため）されるのか…。そこには持前の英語力（言語能力）だけでは対応できない、深く重要な質問が用意されています。ネイティブスピーカーでさえ、おそらくうまく答えられない（説明できない）本質的な問い（テーマ）です。大学に入り、学ぼうとする者にとって、それは避けては通れないテーマになっています。

Unit 2

College Entrance Examinations in the United Kingdom
The Aim of Interviews Focusing on "Who I am"

1 —Precept—

If you desire to enter globally renowned universities like Oxbridge (Oxford and Cambridge), you will need to take an interview test. This oral examination aims to identify who you really are *by assessing your well-balanced academic knowledge and scholarly potentials.*

世界で有名な大学、そう、オックスブリッジ（オックスフォードとケンブリッジ）に入学したいなら、あなたは面接試験（インタビュー）に招待されます。そこではあなたを知るうえで、バランスのとれた学術知識と学究的な潜在能力が見極められることになります。

2 —Prudence and Insight—

イギリスの大学入学試験、とくにオックスフォードやケンブリッジ（通称オックスブリッジ）では筆記試験以外に〈インタビュー〉があります。そこでは「何を重視した質問」が用意されているのか、そのねらいについて話し合ってください。

ヒント（キーワード）：知識力では測れない知性、問題解決能力、分析能力、創造的発想、多面的視点

3 —Understanding the Gist of Each Paragraph of the Main Passage—

Study Focus: College Admission Policy and Required Oral Examination (Interview) in the U.K.

Gist of Each Paragraph

Introduction

[P1] Requirement of interviews in addition to written statements (e.g., Oxbridge).

Body

[P2] Interview—Case 1: Oxford University. Focus on (1) academic potential, motivation, enthusiasm for the selected subject at Oxford, (2) independent creative thinking using new ideas, plus logical thinking.

[P3] Interview—Case 2: Cambridge University. Focus on (1) higher order thinking: applying acquired knowledge to problems in lateral ways.

Conclusion

[P4] Common goal of Oxbridge—assessing overall capabilities that must be competitive and endurable to receive tutorials (Oxford) and supervisions (Cambridge).

[P5] Another common goal—assessing character for the sake of a good human relationship between the tutor/supervisor and the student.

4 —Main Passage and Oral Reading—

[P1] If you are interested in applying for world-renowned top-notch universities like Oxbridge (Oxford and Cambridge Universities), you must take an interview. This oral examination is designed to assess the *quality* of each candidate with focus on *genuine aspects* such as passion for academic learning, ability to seek and explore new ideas through lateral thinking, good insight in grasping facts, information, and situations and interpreting them in uniquely analytical ways. The following excerpts of original information from the two universities provide concrete examples.

[P2] A unique characteristic of an Oxford education is the extensive use of

tutorials[1] or small group sessions between a specialist tutor and one or a few students. These tutorials provide students with the individualized guidance they need to develop their minds both academically and personally. To this end, interviews for Oxford applicants take the form of a mini-tutorial, with specific questions geared towards understanding the academic knowledge as well as analytical skills of the prospective student. Especially, Oxford (composed of 39 different Colleges) looks for "self-motivation and enthusiasm for the subject". The Oxford website assures those who have been invited to an interview to "Feel good!" as they have already made a significant accomplishment by passing the initial screening. A critical aim of the interview is not only to examine interviewees' academic capabilities, but also to confirm their good motivation and passion as mentioned above. What is more, their potential for generating and exercising new ideas in uniquely spontaneous ways is also examined. To prepare for the interview, applicants are recommended to practice "speaking about your subject and your thoughts about what you've seen or read—even if it is with the family cat". Other tips for preparation include "Explore your subject in the wider world", "Take a critical view of ideas and arguments that you encounter in your everyday world" and "Keep practising explaining what you are thinking—almost as if you are thinking out loud". These suggestions point to the fact that careful analysis and self-expression are the most important qualities to demonstrate.

[P3]   Cambridge University is composed of 31 different Colleges, which differ in their course (major) offerings and admission requirements. After a potential student decides the college(s) they wish to apply to, a written application is submitted to each College, or an open application may also be submitted if the student has no special college preference. After the applications are screened, successful candidates are invited to an online or face-to-face interview. This oral examination is discussion-based, and the applicants are asked about their academic areas of interest and relevant particular subjects. Here, the information provided by the applicants in their written statements is utilized as an important supplement. The purpose of this interview is to explore individual applicants' academic potential, motivation and suitability for their selected course and to identify how they exercise higher order thinking, including how they try to apply existing knowledge and skills to unfamiliar problems in lateral ways. Such qualities are essential for a Cambridge education which traditionally uses **supervisions**[2], or small classes with an expert supervisor such as the tutorials at Oxford.

[P4] To summarize, Oxford and Cambridge stress the characteristics of individual interviewees such as their own ideas, uniqueness, and hidden or underdeveloped potentialities. These qualities are indispensable for the study of one's selected course and topic, and in the discussions in tutorials (Oxford) and supervisions (Cambridge). Both Oxford and Cambridge put enormous value on: (1) problem finding, analyzing, solving skills, (2) flexibility when looking into given situations from different angles, (3) voracious interest and passion for confronting difficult questions and issues without losing enthusiasm.

[P5] Also important is (4) *good character*—so that tutors or supervisors can enjoy discussion and dialogue with their selected students. This may be most important in sustaining the traditional legacy of building and sustaining an amicable mentor-mentee relationship at Oxbridge.

[636 words]

語 注

tutorials[1] チュートリアルはオックスフォード大学で 13 世紀に始まった対話型の個別授業。基本的に学部生が対象。学生の興味や関心を深めさせ、知的かつ人間的成長を促していく。チューター（指導者）と学生は 1 対 1 〜 4 の割合で、学生に課したエッセイ（小論文）に批評を加えながら、濃密な議論を毎回おこなう（e.g. 視点や考え方の修正・拡大を目的にしながら）。

supervisions[2] オックスフォード大学のチュートリアルに相当する対話型少人数教育。オックスフォード同様、学部生を対象に毎週実施し、極めて少人数で行う。スーパーバイザー（指導者）は学業面だけでなく、寮生活を含めた大学生活についても指導や助言を行うことがある。

■ Checking Your Oral Reading Speed *Words Per Minute (WPM)*
{Self / Pair / Group}

Measure your WPM using your cellphone or other timing device. Read the passage aloud and determine whether your speed is *sufficient* for reading texts by using the WPM index below.

Words Per Minute (WPM) Index

Total Words ÷ Your Reading Time (in seconds) × 60 = Your WPM
◆ Target WPM = 110 – 125. vs. * *My WPM* = (   )

If your WPM is in the range of the Target WPM, your reading-aloud speed is sufficient to read texts. If your WPM is beyond 125, it is nearing native WPM. If your WPM is below 100, you need to work on your reading speed.

5 —Vocabulary Building—
Important Words / Phrases / Sentences

This vocabulary list contains important words, phrases and sentences from the passage. Using an English-Japanese dictionary or website, please write the Japanese meaning in blank parts.

English	Japanese
[P1]	
in applying for	
world-renowned top-notch	
oral examination is designed to assess	
the *quality* of	
with focus on	
lateral thinking	創造的思考
good insight in grasping facts	事実を把握していく優れた洞察力
[P2]	
the individualized guidance	個別によるガイダンス

develop their minds both academically and personally	学業と一人の人間としての両面から心を育んでいく
to this end	
with specific questions geared towards	... のために（向けられた）絞り込んだ質問
by passing the initial screening	最初の選考過程を通過することで
as mentioned above	上で述べたように
in uniquely spontaneous ways	
other tips for preparation	（面接）準備に向けた別のアドバイス
take a critical view of ideas and arguments	
almost as if you are thinking out loud	まるで声に出して考えているかのように
these suggestions point to the fact that	こうした助言は ... という事実を示している

[P3]

differ in their course (major) offerings and admission requirements	カレッジごとのコース（専攻）の内容と入学要件において異なる
a written application	明記された志願書
an open application	（一部）未確定の志願書
their academic areas of interest and relevant particular subjects	
is utilized as an important supplement	重要な補足資料として使われる
to identify how they exercise higher order thinking	高レベルの思考をどれだけ活用できるかを見極めること
in lateral ways	創造的な方法で
small classes with an expert supervisor	熟練した指導者が行う少人数授業

[P4]

hidden or underdeveloped potentialities	
indispensable for the study of	
put enormous value on	

flexibility when looking into given situations from different angles	与えられた状況をさまざまな角度から探求してく柔軟性
voracious interest and passion	

[P5]

good character

in sustaining the traditional legacy

an amicable mentor-mentee relationship	友好的な師弟関係

<Total: 33 Useful Expressions>

6 —Responsive Writing: In Pursuit of Wider Views and Deeper Thoughts—

From the passage, what point(s) have you gained or learned as good hints for making yourself a *prudent and insightful* person? This *Eureka* (new finding) will become a *good medium* for generating a big question or obtaining new knowledge and findings through discussion with your classmates. Describe your *Eureka* in 100-120 words.

My *Eureka* (New Finding) from the Passage   (   ) words

7 —Note Taking and Exchanging Ideas—Listening Practice and Follow-Up Discussion—

Write down keywords, phrases, or important points from your classmates' presentations on *My Eureka*. Then hold a discussion using this information. Try to raise a big question or obtain further new knowledge through active interaction.

8 —Reflection with a Pure Mind—
素心深考　＊Unit 2 からの学び

　オックスフォード大学は 39 のカレッジ（学寮）、そしてケンブリッジ大学は 31 のカレッジ（学寮）を擁した総合大学で、学寮生活が基本になります。そこでの tutorial または supervision をもとに、密度の濃い学究活動と人間形成が行われます。これをふまえ、知識の豊かさではなく、その知識がどのように縦横無尽な思考とひらめきに応用していけるのか—そこに面接試験（インタビュー）の目的があります。それは 11 世紀設立のオックスフォード、12 世紀設立のケンブリッジが育んできた学風を堅守していくうえで、重要な試験になっています。世界のリーダーとなり、学者となり、あるいは誇れる社会人となって自国と国際社会をけん引していく—面接試験はその入口となっているのかもしれません。

Unit 3

The New Direction of English Learning Motivation Looking into Core Part of Self

1 —Precept—

A foreign language is not just for knowledge acquisition and skill development. Its ontology is also connected with a person's self-growth as a human, as is language learning motivation.

外国語は、知識の獲得とスキル向上のためだけにあるのではない。その存在価値は人間としての自己成長とも結びついている。それは外国語学習の動機づけ（モチベーション）にも言えることだ。

2 —Prudence and Insight—

高校卒業と大学受験を終え、大学で引き続き英語を習っているわけですが、<u>かりに英語圏の大学教授（ネイティブスピーカー）から「あなたにとって英語とは何ですか？」と尋ねられたら</u>、どう答えますか？それについて話し合ってください。あなた自身の考えを述べてみてください。

ヒント（キーワード）：グローバル社会、外国語としての英語、学習目的、英語圏と英語母語話者の世界からかけ離れた学習観

❸ —Understanding the Gist of Each Paragraph of the Main Passage—

Study Focus: Deeper and authentic levels of English learning motivation and language use (Part 1).

Gist of Each Paragraph

Introduction

[P1] Dr. Ema Ushioda is a world-renowned researcher of motivation for learning English as a Foreign Language (EFL). Her motivation theory involves self, identity, society, and life. Feature of the theory—combining the *raison d'être* of a person/human in the world together with the acquisition of EFL while looking into realities and authentic matters in life.

Body

[P2] Definition and explanation of important keywords in the theory, such as *a foreign language, identities, motivation for learning English*.

[P3] Importance of creating self-story (life story) in meaningful ways— searching and using the target language to make the story concrete, while promoting peer interactions.

[P4] Necessity of self-positioning (focusing on present life) and self-orienting (focusing on future life) in an effort to identity "Who I am, what I want to be, what I ought to be as a human being".

[P5] Ushioda's EFL motivation angle—opposite to *Juken*-mode EFL learning.

Conclusion

[P6] To make EFL motivation more realistic and authentic—try to hold a wider and more matured view with focus on improving human society using English.

❹ —Main Passage and Oral Reading—

[P1] Dr. Ema Ushioda is a Professor at University of Warwick in the United Kingdom and a world-renowned researcher of English learning motivation. According to her, in globalized English language education, teachers need to consider more about how to foster each student's identity and personal interest that will lead to successful self-development as a socialized person. In terms of the role and the meaning of English language learning, Dr. Ushioda presents several important messages. They include beneficial hints and implications for Japanese college students—who learn and use English as a foreign language (EFL)—to find out the *raison d'être* of English learning motivation for themselves.

[P2] <u>Dr. Ushioda's Ideas and Implications for Successful EFL Learning and Motivation</u>

- *A foreign language is not simply something to add to our repertoire of skills, but a personalised tool that enables us to expand and express our identity of sense of self in new and interesting ways; to participate in a more diverse range of contexts and broaden our horizons; and to access and share new and alternative sources of information, entertainment or material that we need, value, or enjoy.*

- *While identities are ways of relating the self to the world and are in this sense personally valued constructions, they are socially forged and negotiated through our relations and interactions with other people.*

- *Motivation for learning English is explained not in terms of identification with particular external reference groups (i.e. target language communities or cultures), but identification with an internal representation of how one sees oneself and what one wishes to become.*

[P3] For Dr. Ushioda, self-and-identity perspectives are very important for English learning motivation. For her, it is essential to involve learning experience, interactions (negotiating meaning with classmates and other peer learners), self-development, and creation of a personal history and life story. Such a reality-focused, interpersonal approach can motivate students to challenge the dynamic use of English language.

[P4] As Dr. Ushioda's motivation theory emphasizes human development, it puts value on each person's life history and as a present-future life context. Putting themselves in this chronological framework, English language learners are expected to create their unique life story, which must be personally meaningful and socially challenging. In creating a self-story with a creative mind and critical thinking, the tasks of self-positioning (present) and self-orienting (future) play an important role in identifying "who I am, what I want to be and will be, and what I ought to be" as a person living in society. Dr. Ushioda therefore emphasizes a self-in-society context so that each student can seek the necessary language acquisition for self-development in a tangible manner, which is an inevitable challenge at college level.

[P5]   Dr. Ushioda's ideas of how to learn and use English are fundamentally opposed to *Juken*-mode English learning motivation. Beyond school, classroom, test scores, and grades, she cherishes *authentic reality*. In everyday life, we look at a tug-of-war or battle in business, economy, politics, and other aspects of real society. We also encounter the issue of how to become a good citizen with a proper sense of morality and ethics. College students must prepare to discuss social issues surrounding them on and beyond campus. They need to understand the messages deriving from Dr. Ushioda's motivation theory when considering ongoing social realities.

[P6]   Finally, it is imperative to look at personal matters and social well-being equally in order to make English learning motivation more authentic. College students must figure out what *prosperity* and *well-being* really mean for *healthy* globalization in the contemporary global society, while being mindful of proper citizenship and character formation. As long as we live in a global community, the acquisition of the target language (important words, phrases, sentences of English) will need to overlap with the aim of self-development.

[621 words]

■ Checking Your Oral Reading Speed *Words Per Minute (WPM)*
{Self / Pair / Group}

Measure your WPM using your cellphone or other timing device. Read the passage aloud and determine whether your speed is *sufficient* for reading texts by using the WPM index below.

Words Per Minute (WPM) Index

Total Words ÷ Your Reading Time (in seconds) × 60 = Your WPM
◆　Target WPM = 110 – 125.　vs.　* *My WPM* = (　　　　)

If your WPM is in the range of the Target WPM, your reading-aloud speed is sufficient to read texts. If your WPM is beyond 125, it is nearing native WPM. If your WPM is below 100, you need to work on your reading speed.

5 —Vocabulary Building—
Important Words / Phrases / Sentences

This vocabulary list contains important words, phrases and sentences from the passage. Using an English-Japanese dictionary or website, please write the Japanese meaning in blank parts.

English	Japanese
[P1]	
English learning motivation	英語学習の動機づけ
successful self-development as a socialized person	社会に目を向けた人間としての確かな自己成長
English as a Foreign Language (EFL)	
find out the *raison d'être* of English learning motivation	英語学習動機づけの存在意義を考える
[P2]	
something to add to our repertoire of skills	スキルのレパートリーに加えられるもの
our identity of sense of self	自分という人間の核（アイデンティティ）

22

English	Japanese
in a more diverse range of contexts	より多様な状況に身を置いて
access and share new and alternative sources of	... について新たな代替手段を使って共有していく
ways of relating the self to the world	
personally valued constructions	個人的に価値のある創造物
they are socially forged and negotiated	
identification with particular external reference groups	自分の外の世界に合わせていくという視点
identification with an internal representation of	内面世界（心の動き）に向けた視点

[P3]

English	Japanese
self-and-identity perspectives	自己性とアイデンティティへの展望
negotiating meaning with classmates and other peer learners	クラスメートや他の学習仲間との意味のやりとり
a reality-focused, interpersonal approach	現実をみつめながら他者を介在させていく手法

[P4]

English	Japanese
putting themselves in this chronological framework	この時系列の中にわが身を置きながら
personally meaningful and socially challenging	
the tasks of self-positioning (present) and self-orienting (future)	自分の置かれた立場（現在）と向き合っていく方向づくり（将来）という作業
emphasizes a self-in-society context	社会に自身を投げ込んだ文脈を重視する
in a tangible manner	
an inevitable challenge at college level	

[P5]

English	Japanese
are fundamentally opposed to *Juken*-mode English learning motivation	受験モードの英語学習動機づけとは本質的に離反している
cherishes *authentic reality*	本物の現実感を大切にしている

encounter the issue of how to become a good citizen	善良な市民にどうなっていくべきかという問題も立ちはだかっている
prepare to discuss social issues surrounding them	自分たちを取り巻く社会状況について話し合っていく覚悟をもつ
when considering ongoing social realities	動いている社会の現実を考えた時

[P6]

make English learning motivation more authentic	
figure out what *prosperity* and *well-being* really mean	繁栄と幸福が、実際には何を意味するのかを理解する
while being mindful of proper citizenship and character formation	

<Total: 30 Useful Expressions>

6 —Responsive Writing: In Pursuit of Wider Views and Deeper Thoughts—

From the passage, what point(s) have you gained or learned as good hints for making yourself a *prudent and insightful* person? This *Eureka* (new finding) will become a *good medium* for generating a big question or obtaining new knowledge and findings through discussion with your classmates. Describe your *Eureka* in 100-120 words.

My *Eureka* (New Finding) from the Passage   (   ) words

_____

_____

_____

_____

_____

_____

_____

_____

_____

_____

_____

7 **—Note Taking and Exchanging Ideas—Listening Practice and Follow-Up Discussion—**

Write down keywords, phrases, or important points from your classmates' presentations on *My Eureka*. Then hold a discussion using this information. Try to raise a big question or obtain further new knowledge through active interaction.

8 **—Reflection with a Pure Mind—**
　　素心深考　* Unit 3 からの学び

　英語圏の人々とその社会文化の理解が、高校・中学の英語授業での一つの学習テーマになっています。他方、この外国語学習観は英語母語話者（ネイティブスピーカー）をモデルにし、そこに近づくことが学習成果だと結論づけてしまうかもしれません（けっして誤りではありませんが）。その一方で、このモデル（英語力）に近づけなかったこと、試験でよい成績が得られなかったことが、英語学習のやる気（モチベーション）を低下させる要因ともなっています。そのような外面世界ではなく、ウシオダ博士が述べるように「自分の内なる世界」や「人間としての私」に英語学習のベクトルを向けていく。そこに本当の意味でのモチベーションがあり、それに連動した英語使用体験を蓄積していくことは重要な取り組みと言えます。そこから内発的な動機づけ（intrinsic motivation）が生まれてくるかもしれません。

Unit 4

Teaching and Learning English in the Era of Globalization
Ontology of a Foreign Language

1 —Precept—

"What is the aim of learning English?" To answer this question, it is important to examine and prescribe how the language learning practice will fit into one's personal beliefs and sense of values. Such inner spirituality acts as the starting point for sustainable motivation.

「英語を学ぶ目的は何だろう？」これに答えるには、語学の実践が自分の信念と価値観にどうフィットしているかを精査し、処方していくことが大切になる。そのような内面的で深い精神部分が、持続可能で優れたモチベーションづくりへの出発点となる。

2 —Prudence and Insight—

"モチベーション（動機づけ）"がスポーツをはじめ、さまざまな分野で使われています。では「英語学習のモチベーションを自分はどのように高めているのか？」－その取り組みについて学習目的や方法を含めながら話し合ってください。大学受験が終わり、英語へのモチベーションをどこに向けていけばよいのか？大学卒業後の人生までを意識した、持続可能なモチベーションを確立できているのか？大きな視点に立ちながら話し合ってください。

ヒント（キーワード）：英語学習の再定義、教室やテストをこえた動機づけ、大学がもつ社会的使命と連動した英語学習の目的、注目される（外国語としての）英語モチベーション理論の内容

3 —Understanding the Gist of Each Paragraph of the Main Passage—

Study Focus: Deeper and authentic levels of English learning motivation and language use (Part 2).

Gist of Each Paragraph

Introduction

[P1]   The role of the English language in globalization, along with the perspective of English teaching and learning motivation. Also, the goal of using English among college students with focus on how to explain their *raison d'être* in a precise manner in accordance with Dr. Ema Ushioda's worldview (continued from Unit 3).

Body

[P2]   Brief review—research history of motivation for learning English as a foreign language (EFL).

[P3]   New trend in EFL learning motivation—equal emphasis on successful description of oneself as a socially responsible person and successful description of personal beliefs and sense of values as a core part of self and identity.

[P4]   A shared important connection between personal motivation and goals of college education—good character formation (successful self-growth) as a person. Here, *ontology, teleology, and axiology* with focus on a person's philosophy of life are crucially relevant aspects.

[P5]   Dr. Ushioda's ideas of successful EFL learning motivation, including *the meaning of learning English, the role of the language classroom, and the definition of success*.

Conclusion

[P6]   Wider, insightful views of Dr. Ushioda's motivation theory—expecting the enhancement of self-esteem and self-efficacy through knowing oneself in the real world and by using English for this aim. The ultimate success lies in becoming a mature person (EFL learner) who can think, judge, decide, then act autonomously.

4 —Main Passage and Oral Reading—

[P1] As history witnesses, the English language has played a vital role in promoting globalization. Parallel to this movement, the goal of English teaching has been oriented towards promoting language learning motivation of school students. Meanwhile, college students are more and more urged to describe their *raison d'être* in a precise manner using English. This educational trend has also become a new trend of English learning motivation, as Dr. Ema Ushioda suggested (Unit 3).

[P2] Traditionally, motivation for learning English as a foreign language (EFL) has been confined to a limited scope, such as getting good exam scores, studying abroad, or communicating with native speakers from English-speaking countries. It then progressed to speaking with assistant language teachers (ALTs) in the classroom, watching movies and listening to songs in English. However, English as a mode for self-expression of one's own beliefs and values is still rare.

[P3] In contrast, a new authentic EFL motivation is associated with the challenge and accomplishment of describing *who I am and what I will be and what I ought to be as a socially responsible human being*. It emphasizes students' internal self-development by focusing on personal beliefs and sense of values. In this context, traditional and conventional educational methods such as studying textbooks and emphasizing *correct* answers do not make sense, and limited answers prepared by the instructor may not be workable or beneficial. Instead of worrying about test results, it is much more important to be able to explain your goals and convictions in your own English.

[P4] The mission of college English, together with the aim of college education, lies in supporting good character development, that is, successful self-growth as a human being. This philosophy therefore pays attention to *ontology* (clarifying each person/student's *raison d'être*), *teleology* (clarifying life goals), and *axiology* (fixing and stabilizing beliefs and values). Dr. Ushioda suggests relevant messages below, which are aimed at understanding language learning motivation and subsequent learning strategy.

[P5] <u>Dr. Ushioda's Ideas and Implications for Successful EFL Learning Motivation (Continued from Unit 3)</u>

- Students need to consider *what English and learning English mean to them, and to examine the ambivalences and complexities of how they see English fitting into (or not fitting into) their personal system of values, goals and identities, now that learning English for exams no longer provides a prescribed rationale.*
- *The classroom functions as a microcosm of the larger social world and should mirror its democratic and co-operative structures. In this sense, arguments about the socially embedded and political dimensions of motivation apply just as much to language learning and use in the classroom setting.*
- *From a pedagogical perspective, ... we should encourage our students to view the target language as a means of self-expression and self-development. In other words, we need to engage their own identities and interests in our lessons and promote a sense of continuity between what they learn and do in the classroom, and who they are and what they are interested in doing in their lives outside the classroom, now and in the future.*
- *Success should be defined in terms that are transparently meaningful to the student, if our intent is to foster self-sustaining intrinsic motivational processes, rather than the short-term motivational processes that depend on regular external incentives or pressures, such as teachers' marks, class tests, etc.*

[P6]   To reiterate, Dr. Ushioda consistently emphasizes the realm of self and identity and real society. Seeking authenticity, her motivation theory is also concerned with possible emergence of self-esteem and self-efficacy (i.e., developing good self-pride-and-confidence) in learning and using English. In eliciting this, however, aspirations and resolutions are crucial, in particular for solidifying each person's selfhood (personal beliefs and values and philosophy of life). Focusing on one's inner spiritual self and matury becomes important for guiding students to become self-motivated, self-directed, self-determined, and self-responsible EFL learners. Consequently, *being matured enough to become autonomous* is the final goal of EFL motivation.

[650 words]

■ Checking Your Oral Reading Speed *Words Per Minute (WPM)*
{Self / Pair / Group}

Measure your WPM using your cellphone or other timing device. Read the passage aloud and determine whether your speed is *sufficient* for reading texts by using the WPM index below.

Words Per Minute (WPM) Index

Total Words ÷ Your Reading Time (in seconds) × 60 = Your WPM

◆ Target WPM = 110 – 125. vs. * *My WPM* = (   )

If your WPM is in the range of the Target WPM, your reading-aloud speed is sufficient to read texts. If your WPM is beyond 125, it is nearing native WPM. If your WPM is below 100, you need to work on your reading speed.

5 —Vocabulary Building—
Important Words / Phrases / Sentences

This vocabulary list contains important words, phrases and sentences from the passage. Using an English-Japanese dictionary or website, please write the Japanese meaning in blank parts.

English	Japanese
[P1]	
parallel to this movement	この動きに合わせて
meanwhile	
to describe their *raison d'être* in a precise manner	自分の存在意義をより詳しく述べていく
[P2]	
has been confined to a limited scope	
[P3]	
is associated with the challenge and accomplishment of	... に挑み、やり遂げていくことと連動している
internal self-development	内面からの自己成長
personal beliefs and sense of values	

limited answers prepared by the instructor	教員が用意している限られた答え（正解）

[P4]

the mission of ... lies in supporting good character development	... の真の目的はすぐれた人格の育成にかかっている

ontology
teleology
axiology

[P5]

personal system of values, goals and identities	個人的な価値観、目標、アイデンティティの枠組み
no longer provides a prescribed rationale	十分に処方された、理論的根拠を与えてはくれない
functions as a microcosm of	... の縮図として機能する
mirror its democratic and co-operative structures	民主的で協力的な空間として機能していく
the socially embedded and political dimensions of motivation	社会に密着し、政治的な側面ももつ動機づけ
from a pedagogical perspective	
view the target language as a means of self-expression and self-development	
engage their own identities and interests	自身のアイデンティティと興味を持ち込む
promote a sense of continuity	
transparently meaningful	
foster self-sustaining intrinsic motivational processes	自ら維持していこうとする内発的な動機づけプロセス
regular external incentives or pressures	定期的な外からの誘発や圧力

[P6]

is also concerned with possible emergence of self-esteem and self-efficacy	自己肯定感と自己効力感が出てくる可能性とも関係している
solidifying each person's selfhood	
one's inner spiritual self and maturity	自分の内にある心の部分ならびに成熟

| self-motivated, self-directed, self-determined, and self-responsible EFL learners | 自らを動機づけて自発的になり、自己決定を下し、自己責任をとっていく英語学習者 |

<Total: 28 Useful Expressions>

6 —Responsive Writing: In Pursuit of Wider Views and Deeper Thoughts—

From the passage, what point(s) have you gained or learned as good hints for making yourself a *prudent and insightful* person? This *Eureka* (new finding) will become a *good medium* for generating a big question or obtaining new knowledge and findings through discussion with your classmates. Describe your *Eureka* in 100-120 words.

My *Eureka* (New Finding) from the Passage　　　　　(　　) **words**

_____

_____

_____

_____

_____

_____

_____

_____

_____

_____

_____

7 —Note Taking and Exchanging Ideas—Listening Practice and Follow-Up Discussion—

Write down keywords, phrases, or important points from your classmates' presentations on *My Eureka*. Then hold a discussion using this information. Try to raise a big question or obtain further new knowledge through active interaction.

8 —Reflection with a Pure Mind—
素心深考　＊Unit 4 からの学び

　（外国語としての）英語動機づけ理論において、ウシオダ博士（アイルランド人、英国ウォーリック大学教授）には「こだわり」があります。ぶれずにしぼまない本当の動機づけのあり方―この動機づけの正統化に向けて "a foreign language" をはじめ、motivation に関わる重要キーワードに目をつけ、その定義を明確にしています。それによって「英語の存在論（ontology）」を明らかにしようとしています。いずれは実社会に出ていくという現実。長い道のりを生き抜いていくという人生の現実。この文脈にわが身とわが英語（学習）を交錯させたとき、確かに応えてくれる英語学習のモチベーションの姿が映し出されてくる ...。ウシオダ博士の動機づけ理論はそこに向かっています。

Unit 5

Mission and Purpose of College Education
Cherishing Eternal Truths

1 —Precept—

Knowledge leading to sound judgment cannot be learned nor obtained only through reading textbooks and taking lectures. Rather, this knowledge is fostered through the explicit mission and traditional educational policy embraced by the university.

健全な判断力につながる知識は、教科書を読んで講義を受けただけでは獲得できない。むしろこの知識は、大学が抱く明確な使命と伝統的な教育理念を通して育まれる。

2 —Prudence and Insight—

大学に入学した理由や目的は、在籍している学部や学科（専攻分野）と大きく関係しています。その一方で、専門知識とスキルの獲得だけが大学教育の目的ではありません。そのような能力主義（コンピテンシー中心）的な世界とは別に、いかなる大切なものを米国の大学は独自の教育理念をもとに重視しているのか？それについて話し合ってください。

ヒント（キーワード）：現実社会が求める人間的資質、市民性、正義、美徳

3 —Understanding the Gist of Each Paragraph of the Main Passage—

Study Focus: Traditional value of college education.

Gist of Each Paragraph

Introduction

[P1]   The mission of higher education—development of good character and good citizenship.

Body

[P2]   Relevant source 1: The educational goal and school philosophy of Harvard University. A key phrase is "The Transformative Power of a Liberal Arts and Sciences Education". This mission statement emphasizes the students' commitment and effort for self-transformation (i.e., being a more matured person). To this end, liberal arts and sciences should be meaningfully studied and integrated into students' lives, thus leading to the realization of the attainment of a more just, fair, and promising world.

[P3]   Relevant source 2: A lecture at University of Chicago by Dr. John W. Boyer, a distinguished professor of history. As at Harvard, his emphasis is on the importance of liberal education, that is, the empowerment of critical thinking, writing, and argumentation skills.

[P4]   Relevant source 3: A statement by Professor Ernest Boyer. He argues that fostering knowledge and skill for *sound judgment* is important in the journey of identifying *Who I am, What is my purpose of life, and What is the true meaning of success*.

[P5]   Value judgments of "what is right/wrong", "what is meaningful/ meaningless", "what is valuable/not valuable" are authentic topics of discussion in college education.

[P6]   Relevant source 4: A statement by Professor Anne Colby. She argues that virtue, morality, ethics cannot be excluded or ignored in sound judgment and in citizenship education.

Conclusion

[P7]   In fostering college students' keen sense of socialization, teaching and learning about values (value judgments) plays an important role.

[P1]   Concerning school missions and educational goals, all universities cherish at least one core value; that is, accepting, nurturing, and empowering undergraduate students to be good people and good citizens. This overarching policy dictates each school's *raison d'être*, particularly regarding good character development and good citizenship.

[P2]   Take the example in case of Harvard University. With a view to realizing convincing self-growth and good citizenship, the Harvard website articulates its educational philosophy termed *"The Transformative Power of a Liberal Arts and Sciences Education."* There, the emphasis is put on the nurture of competent future leaders contributing to the emergence of a fair and just society. A critical mission of Harvard lies in fostering and empowering good citizenship. This lofty aim is achieved through extensive commitment and efforts aimed to functionalize the transformative power of a good education in liberal arts and sciences. Accordingly, Harvard's vision is to provide learning environments in which students can learn, experience, and appreciate a dynamic "unparalleled educational journey that is intellectually, socially, and personally transformative". Such an academic policy plays a vital part in realizing *authentic* transformative power not only of self but also society at large.

[P3]   At the University of Chicago, Dr. John W. Boyer, a distinguished professor of history, gave a lecture on the mission of college education. There, he addressed the importance of general education (i.e., liberal arts and sciences), as it constitutes the fundamental principle of *liberal learning* (e.g., challenging, developing, empowering various learning practices that encompass creativity, critique, analysis, investigation, reflection, etc.). In other words, education for liberal learning (i.e., liberal studies) is indispensable in higher education as it aims to help students acquire core academic skills such as writing, critical thinking, and argumentation. In Dr. Boyer's eyes, the ultimate goal of liberal education is to help college students become capable of posing questions boldly and convincingly. After graduation, this self-confidence will become the seed of a lifelong inquisitive mind and an enriched social life.

[P4]   College professor Ernest LeRoy Boyer (September 13, 1928–December

8, 1995) explained why the undergraduate period is so important in his book *College: The Undergraduate Experience in America* (1987). Dr. Boyer argued that fostering knowledge and skill for *sound judgment* is important in searching and identifying *Who I am, What is my purpose of life, and What is the true meaning of success.*

[P5]   Throughout history, value judgments of "what is right/wrong", "what is meaningful/meaningless", "what is beneficial/unbeneficial" and "what is valuable/not valuable" have been authentic topics of study and discussion in college education. This is because, after graduation, students must face and tackle complex and difficult problems, mostly arising from a diversified human society, even in local communities and regions.

[P6]   Professor Anne Colby at Stanford University argues the importance of fostering a civic mind and promoting civic engagement during the undergraduate period. In her co-authored book *Educating Citizens: Preparing America's Undergraduates for Lives of Moral and Civic Responsibility* (2003), Dr. Colby emphasized the necessity of empowering judgmental skills, especially when struggling with tough situations and complicated incidents. This is because in reality, different values and beliefs intersect and conflict with each other. Furthermore, virtue, morality, ethics, and other *abstract and elusive* concepts are more likely to be involved in such cases, thus making situations more difficult and complex to negotiate. Moreover, during negotiations, individual persons' beliefs and values may well be involved in judgment and final decision-making.

[P7]   Consequently, undergraduates must improve their critical thinking, writing and argumentation skills. They also need to be proactive in presenting bold questions. These actions must be the pillar of liberal education and liberal learning at college. For college students, it is imperative to strengthen a keen sense of socialization and demonstrate civic virtues. As articulated in the introduction, Harvard has never ignored or downplayed this aspect, thus conveying this message: "Toward a more just, fair, and promising world".

[637 words]

■ Checking Your Oral Reading Speed **Words Per Minute (WPM)**
{Self / Pair / Group}

Measure your WPM using your cellphone or other timing device. Read the passage aloud and determine whether your speed is *sufficient* for reading texts by using the WPM index below.

Words Per Minute (WPM) Index

Total Words ÷ Your Reading Time (in seconds) × 60 = Your WPM
◆ Target WPM = 110 – 125.   vs. * *My WPM* = (   )

If your WPM is in the range of the Target WPM, your reading-aloud speed is sufficient to read texts. If your WPM is beyond 125, it is nearing native WPM. If your WPM is below 100, you need to work on your reading speed.

5 —Vocabulary Building—
Important Words / Phrases / Sentences

This vocabulary list contains important words, phrases and sentences from the passage. Using an English-Japanese dictionary or website, please write the Japanese meaning in blank parts.

English	Japanese
[P1]	
cherish at least one core value	核となる価値を少なからず大切にしている
each school's *raison d'être*	各大学の存在意義
good character development and good citizenship	
[P2]	
with a view to realizing convincing self-growth and good citizenship	確かな自己成長と善良な市民精神の実現に向け
articulates its educational philosophy termed	...という教育哲学（教育理念）を掲げている

The Transformative Power of a Liberal Arts and Sciences Education	リベラルアーツと科学系の教育がもたらす変革力
the emergence of a fair and just society	公正と正義による社会の実現
a critical mission	
this lofty aim is achieved through	この崇高な目的は… によって達成される
functionalize the transformative power of a good education	
unparalleled educational journey	織り込まれた教育の旅
plays a vital part in	
[P3]	
a distinguished professor of history	
the importance of general education	
the fundamental principle of *liberal learning*	自由な学びの基本原則
indispensable in higher education	高等教育（大学教育）では不可欠となる
become capable of posing questions boldly and convincingly	大胆に確信をもって質問していける
become the seed of a lifelong inquisitive mind	生涯にわたる探究心への元となる
[P4]	
fostering knowledge and skill for *sound judgment*	
[P5]	
value judgments	
authentic topics of study and discussion	
students must face and tackle	学生たちは ... に直面しながら取り組んでいかなければならない
arising from a diversified human society	
[P6]	
fostering a civic mind and promoting civic engagement	市民感覚を育て、市民参加を高めていく
empowering judgmental skills	

when struggling with tough situations and complicated incidents	
different values and beliefs intersect and conflict with each other	異なる価値観や信念が交錯し、対立している
abstract and elusive concepts	抽象的で捉えづらい概念
[P7]	
need to be proactive in	
strengthen a keen sense of socialization	社会化（社会づくり）という感覚を磨いていく
demonstrate civic virtues	
has never ignored or downplayed this aspect	

<Total: 32 Useful Expressions>

6 —Responsive Writing: In Pursuit of Wider Views and Deeper Thoughts—

From the passage, what point(s) have you gained or learned as good hints for making yourself a *prudent and insightful* person? This *Eureka* (new finding) will become a *good medium* for generating a big question or obtaining new knowledge and findings through discussion with your classmates. Describe your *Eureka* in 100-120 words.

My *Eureka* (New Finding) from the Passage ( ) **words**

_____

_____

_____

_____

_____

_____

_____

_____

_____

_____

7 —Note Taking and Exchanging Ideas—Listening Practice and Follow-Up Discussion—

Write down keywords, phrases, or important points from your classmates' presentations on *My Eureka*. Then hold a discussion using this information. Try to raise a big question or obtain further new knowledge through active interaction.

8 —Reflection with a Pure Mind—
素心深考　＊Unit 5 からの学び

　欧米の大学で何十世紀もの間、大切に守られ、受け継がれている精神。それは「そもそも論」（本質性に目を向け、明らかにしていく学問姿勢）へのまなざしです。そもそも大学で学ぶとは何を意味するのか？そもそも在学中に自分自身と向き合い、自らに問いかけ、考えるべきことは何なのか...。溢れかえる情報、人、モノの流れに振り回されないよう、冷静なマインドで「質の高いそもそも論」を自分に仕掛けていくことは大切です。その真実を学生たちに知ってもらうことが大学教育の変わらぬ使命とも言えます。すぐに飛びついてしまう「とにかく論」から自分を遠ざけていくためにも ...。

Unit **6**

Unchanging Values at the University
In Consideration of Good Character and Good Society

1 —Precept—

It is a great pity whenever precious experiences of confronting, tackling, and appreciating great ideas and views in college education and for character education are lost due to intensified competition and crass assessment.

激しい競争とあからさまな評価により、偉大な思想と視点と出会い、格闘し、深く理解していく貴重な体験が奪われていくとしたら、それは大学教育と人格教育において深い悲しみとなろう。

2 —Prudence and Insight—

　トップクラスに位置する伝統ある有名大学は「エリート校」と呼ばれています。そこでの教育方針は驕りや偏った自尊感情を植えつけていくことではありません。世の中を正しい方向へ先導していくリーダーとしての使命感と責務、そして円熟した市民性が重視されています。米国のアイビーリーグ校（ハーバードを含む、8校からなる有名私立大学）の教育精神はこの点に立っています。その1つであるブラウン大学の場合、どのような教育文化を守ろうとしているのか、それについて考えてみてください。

ヒント（キーワード）：物欲と金儲けと競争主義からの脱皮、大学文化として継承すべき人間関係、人としての幸福の原点、価値（判断）教育

3 **—Understanding the Gist of Each Paragraph of the Main Passage—**

Study Focus: Brown Curriculum and Brown Spirit—The Legacy of Brown University.

Gist of Each Paragraph

Introduction

[P1] Brief explanation of Brown University (an Ivy League School) with its prominent features and notable points, including the uniqueness of the "Brown Curriculum".

[P2] University President Ruth Simmons' brief profile, including her brilliant successes (i.e., selected and named "America's best college president" and "Ms. Woman of the Year in 2002") and her inaugural speech emphasizing the excellent points of Brown University's education centered on character, human relationships, and values.

Body

[P3] Her focus 1: The eternal mission of college education, together with the importance of teaching values (i.e., importance of acquiring the knowledge and skill of good judgment as a college student).

[P4] Her focus 2: The traditional legacy of Brown University (Brown Community)—good relationship between teachers and students while both enjoy rewarding intellectual experiences.

[P5] Her focus 3: Another honorable part of school culture—avoiding and downplaying overheated competition and crass assessment endemic to colleges today. Instead, Brown emphasizes preparing students to become joyful, intelligent, humane and concerned adults before graduation.

[P6] Her focus 4: Her definition of poverty based on her personal experience.

Conclusion

[P7] Her educational philosophy and warning: Reconsider the unchanging and never-ending mission of higher education. It should never be driven by the business of gold-chasing (money-making) at the expense of successful character formation and meaningful campus life.

4 —Main Passage and Oral Reading—

[P1] Brown University in Providence, Rhode Island, was founded in 1764. It is the seventh-oldest university in the United States and belongs to the Ivy League. Brown is the first American college that accepted students regardless of their background or religious affiliation. In 1969, Brown adopted a new curriculum (called "Brown Curriculum") which enabled students to be *the architects of their own syllabus*. This curriculum eliminated mandatory course requirements in general education, allowing students to take any course for a grade of satisfactory (Pass) or no-credit (Fail). Admissions are among the most selective in the United States, with an acceptance rate of about 7% in 2019.

[P2] Dr. Ruth Simmons, the 18th president of Brown University, was selected "America's best college president" by *TIME* magazine in 2001, also selected "Ms. Woman of the Year in 2002" by *NewsWeek* magazine. She was the first African American president in the Ivy League schools. Upon taking this honorable position, President Simmons delivered her inaugural speech. There, she addressed the traditional legacy of Brown University, together with her beliefs on good character development, good human relationships, and good values for a brighter Brown community. The following quotes reflect such significant ideas, and they tell us about what *University Wisdom* means beyond fashions and social movements.

[P3] President's Address to Brown University Community

Good afternoon. I am delighted to have the opportunity to lead this outstanding University in this exciting time in history. I was recently asked whether universities should teach values. My response was that universities, whether implicitly or otherwise, always, always teach values. The values that Brown implicitly teaches its students are manifest in its open curriculum, in the way the University stresses individual responsibility, in the value the University places on commitment to community involvement and civic engagement, and in its acknowledged recognition of the need for diversity in both social relations and intellectual choices.

[P4] Bound together as learners and mentors, apprentices and guides, and colleagues and friends, Brown faculty and students have the privilege of an intensely rewarding intellectual experience built not just on a dominant-subordinate model of education, nor on crude competitive antics, nor on arrogant elitism, but on a deep and genuine mutual regard for different intellectual ends and approaches. Those who enter this environment face high expectations, but they receive the highest rewards at the end of their journey.

[P5]　Most importantly, in an age when the core purpose of education is often lost in a miasma of competition and crass assessment and where the raw experience of confronting great and enduring ideas grows rare, the Brown curriculum helps to restore, I think, the elemental relationship between ideas and the human spirit. And is that not the noblest purpose of education? I rather think so. The Brown student is legendary and is, by many accounts, the most appealing in the country. Joyful and intelligent, humane and concerned, Brown students are said to be the happiest and the most balanced in the Ivy League.

[P6]　I am here because of my parents, but I am also here because of ... unknown donors. They helped me to understand something very important: that poverty is not a state of mind nor a definition of one's character, but merely the condition of one's purse. I think it is the duty of education at every level to care about the opportunity for children of limited resources to establish an intimate relationship with ideas and high ideals.

[P7]　Higher education today is caught in an ever-widening dilemma in which silver and gold dominate our thinking and our planning. In the lure of this gold are the seeds of irrelevance, self-satisfaction and loss of public trust. Universities exist not to amass wealth but to release minds and to amass knowledge. Brown must fix and stay its course and not imitate the gold chase of so many in higher education today.

[639 words]

■ Checking Your Oral Reading Speed *Words Per Minute (WPM)*
{Self / Pair / Group}

Measure your WPM using your cellphone or other timing device. Read the passage aloud and determine whether your speed is *sufficient* for reading texts by using the WPM index below.

Words Per Minute (WPM) Index

Total Words ÷ Your Reading Time (in seconds) × 60 = Your WPM

◆ Target WPM = 110 – 125. vs. * *My WPM* = (   )

If your WPM is in the range of the Target WPM, your reading-aloud speed is sufficient to read texts. If your WPM is beyond 125, it is nearing native WPM. If your WPM is below 100, you need to work on your reading speed.

5 —Vocabulary Building—
Important Words / Phrases / Sentences

This vocabulary list contains important words, phrases and sentences from the passage. Using an English-Japanese dictionary or website, please write the Japanese meaning in blank parts.

English	Japanese
[P1]	
the *architects of their own syllabus*	自らが「シラバスの設計者」となる
eliminated mandatory course requirements in general education	一般教育の必修科目（数）を削減した
a grade of satisfactory (Pass) or no-credit (Fail)	単位を認める（合格）か不認定（不合格）とする成績評価
[P2]	
delivered her inaugural speech	自身の就任演説を行った
beyond fashions and social movements	

[P3]

whether universities should teach values 　　大学で価値観というものを教
　　　　　　　　　　　　　　　　　　　　えるべきかどうか

whether implicitly or otherwise 　　示唆を含む、またはそれ以外
　　　　　　　　　　　　　　　　　　　の方法を採ろうとも

manifest in its open curriculum 　　... はオープンカリキュラム
　　　　　　　　　　　　　　　　　　の中に表れている

commitment to community involvement and 　　地域への参画と市民として関
　　civic engagement 　　　　　　　　　　わっていく
the need for diversity in both social relations
　　and intellectual choices
[P4]

bound together as 　　... という（としての）絆を
　　　　　　　　　　　　　　　もつ

an intensely rewarding intellectual experience 　　密度が濃く、手応えのある知
　　　　　　　　　　　　　　　　　　　　　　的経験

a dominant-subordinate model of education 　　教育のタテ関係（支配—隷
　　　　　　　　　　　　　　　　　　　　従）

crude competitive antics 　　あからさまな競争心
arrogant elitism
different intellectual ends and approaches 　　さまざまな知の目的と方法
[P5]

in a miasma of competition and crass assess- 　　競争と粗っぽい評価の波に飲
　　ment 　　　　　　　　　　　　　　み込まれている
the raw experience of confronting great and 　　偉大で永続的な思想にふれて
　　enduring ideas grows rare 　　　　いく生の経験
by many accounts 　　よく聞く話として
joyful and intelligent, humane and concerned
[P6]

not a state of mind nor a definition of one's 　　心の状態や人の性格をさすも
　　character 　　　　　　　　　　　　　のではなく
merely the condition of one's purse
children of limited resources 　　限られた資源（金銭状況）の
　　　　　　　　　　　　　　　　　　　中で生きていく子供たち

an intimate relationship with ideas and high
　　ideals

50

[P7]

silver and gold dominate our thinking and our planning	銀と金（金儲け）に支配された考えや計画
not to amass wealth but to release minds and to amass knowledge	富を蓄える場ではなく、人の心を解き放ち、知識を豊かにする
imitate the gold chase	金儲け主義に追従していく
in higher education today	

<Total: 28 Useful Expressions>

6 —Responsive Writing: In Pursuit of Wider Views and Deeper Thoughts—

From the passage, what point(s) have you gained or learned as good hints for making yourself a *prudent and insightful* person? This *Eureka* (new finding) will become a *good medium* for generating a big question or obtaining new knowledge and findings through discussion with your classmates. Describe your *Eureka* in 100-120 words.

My *Eureka* (New Finding) from the Passage   **(**   **) words**

7 **—Note Taking and Exchanging Ideas—Listening Practice and Follow-Up Discussion—**

Write down keywords, phrases, or important points from your classmates' presentations on *My Eureka*. Then hold a discussion using this information. Try to raise a big question or obtain further new knowledge through active interaction.

8 **—Reflection with a Pure Mind—**
素心深考　* Unit 6 からの学び

　「価値観」といえば聞こえはよさそうですが、そこにはややもすると私利私欲、主観、偏狭な視点が宿っている可能性があります。そういったエゴ的な世界から抜け出し、深みのある価値観形成が大学時代に求められています。たとえば「公共レベル」に目を向けた価値観づくりです。これについて、世界トップクラスの大学ではヒドゥンカリキュラム（hidden curriculum：表には出て来ないカリキュラム）を通して取り組んでいます。それは正規の教育カリキュラムと同様に重視されています。そこには単位取得や成績では推し量れない、真の「学修成果」に対するこだわりが宿っています。建学精神、校是、学風といった自校のプライドを賭けた教育を推し進めるうえでも、価値観づくりと健全な判断能力は重要な教育目標になっています。

Unit **7**

College Commencement
An Authentic Life Ritual

1 —Precept—

When you attend college commencement, remember that it is an important life ritual before you launch into your new life in a new world.

　大学卒業式への参列... 覚えておくがいい。それは新たな世界と人生の門出に向けた、重要な人生儀式の場であることを。

2 —Prudence and Insight—

　大学卒業式とは単なるイベントではありません。米国の場合、それは荘厳、壮麗、優美、そして厳粛なオーラに包まれています（気の利いたエスプリやユーモアを交えながら）。それは「人生の通過儀式（イニシエーション）」であるという考えが、伝統的に継承されています。単位修得、科目履修、成績の優劣をこえた「人間としての成長、つまり成熟した内面世界」の完成度を確認し、そこまでの軌跡を振り返る儀式の場となっています。この点をふまえ、学長や招かれた著名人が用意したメッセージにはどのような内容が込められているのか、話し合ってください。

ヒント（キーワード）：米国で重んじられている価値観、内面的成熟の証明、社会人としての心得、人生の成功の究極的な意味

3 —Understanding the Gist of Each Paragraph of the Main Passage—

Study Focus: What needs to be confirmed at the end of college life.

Gist of Each Paragraph

Introduction

[P1] The role and mission of college commencement and the content of commencement addresses.

[P2] The *raison d'être* of the commencement as a sacred *life ritual*.

Body

[P3] Analysis of commencement speeches—content can be divided into several categories. For instance, (1) precepts indicating the importance of human society and human networks.

[P4] (2) precepts emphasizing character formation as a human being.

[P5] (3) precepts about self and identity, self-growth and self-enlightenment for success in life.

[P6] (4) precepts highlighting inner spirituality and philosophy.

Conclusion

[P7] A college commencement is a sacred ceremony. Attending and listening attentively to the commencement addresses is imperative to recognize their contents as *good aphorisms* before launching into real society and contributing to it as a matured citizen.

4 —Main Passage and Oral Reading—

[P1] A college commencement address is a sort of *jewel*, specifically geared to remind graduating students about what they have learned, discussed, explored, and achieved as precious learning outcomes in their university lives. All learned experiences are meaningful and useful, and thus should be applied in a new life stage after college graduation.

[P2] College commencement is not a simple ceremony but a sacred *life ritual*. In it, various thought-provoking messages are created and imparted by school authorities and invited celebrities. Overall, their conveyed messages are likely to emphasize truth, duty, mission, and responsibility as a human being—in sum, simple matters of utmost importance of human life. They also focus on good character, good society, true happiness—all of which are beyond materialism and egocentrism.

[P3]   The messages of commencement speeches can be divided into several categories. For instance, the following messages are oriented towards human societies and human networks.

- If you don't participate in society and try to identify values and set priorities there, it will be difficult to recognize a sense of reality and your place in society.

- It is difficult to understand your own life practically, if you lack the ability to grasp the world on a large scale, surpassing your personal life, your residence, and your home country.

- Never forget this fact—whether working in a small place or at a large company, you are always connected and supported by others—your colleagues, supervisors, friends and neighbors.

[P4]   For character forming, the following messages are worthwhile noting.

- Your character will not become authentic unless it is embellished with integrity and wisdom.

- The quality of character will never tarnish, while material possessions easily rust and fade away and depreciate in the end.

- Character forming is a life-long process, and it can happen at any time, in any place, and on any occasion. Therefore, be flexible and open-minded in accepting various opportunities and circumstances without prejudice, subjectivity or self-righteousness.

[P5]   In terms of self, identity, and self-growth-and-enlightenment, the following messages are attractive.

- What is life? What is it for? A solid answer is it exists to teach you "Who I am, What I want to be, and What I ought to be."

- What is identity? This core part of self can never be established or authenticated without putting yourself in difficult situations then encouraging yourself to seek convincing answers.

- Be open to receiving vicissitudes of life. This mindset entices you into wisdom.

[P6] As to one's inner spiritual part (spirituality) and philosophy, the following messages are interesting.

- Remember that bravery is the most important virtue in practical wisdom. Being brave is an act, not a thought, so show it in concrete ways.
- As people live longer, subconsciously or unconsciously, they tend to put the highest priority and value on money making. However, as long as you stick to this game, you will forget one important thing and will be shocked by this simple question: "Who am I? What is my *raison d'être*?"
- Always try to stop, examine and reflect upon your life motto or philosophy of life. Modify and reconstruct it by examining your beliefs and sense of values with critical eyes. Otherwise, you will be easily swayed and sink in the waves of social movements, and you will try to avoid social pressures in vain.

[P7] College commencement is a sacred ceremony. Attending college commencement and listening to commencement addresses is the final event of academic learning. In them, the prepared messages act as *good aphorisms* for college graduates, making their whole college lives brilliant. Needless to say, heartfelt considerations and sincere desires are inscribed in the aphorisms for the sake of new college graduates, along with prayers for real success and true happiness in life.

[625 words]

■ Checking Your Oral Reading Speed   *Words Per Minute (WPM)*
{Self / Pair / Group}

Measure your WPM using your cellphone or other timing device. Read the passage aloud and determine whether your speed is *sufficient* for reading texts by using the WPM index below.

Words Per Minute (WPM) Index

Total Words ÷ Your Reading Time (in seconds) × 60 = Your WPM
◆   Target WPM = 110 – 125. vs. * *My WPM* = (   )

If your WPM is in the range of the Target WPM, your reading-aloud speed is sufficient to read texts. If your WPM is beyond 125, it is nearing native WPM. If your WPM is below 100, you need to work on your reading speed.

5 —Vocabulary Building—
Important Words / Phrases / Sentences

This vocabulary list contains important words, phrases and sentences from the passage. Using an English-Japanese dictionary or website, please write the Japanese meaning in blank parts.

English	Japanese
[P1]	
a college commencement address	
geared to remind graduating students about	卒業生たちに... を想起させるうえで
should be applied in a new life stage	
[P2]	
a sacred *life ritual*	
various thought-provoking messages	考えさせられるさまざまなメッセージ
school authorities and invited celebrities	
beyond materialism and egocentrism	物質主義と自己中心主義をこえた
[P3]	
the following messages are oriented towards	次のメッセージは... に向けられている
identity values and set priorities	価値観や優先順位をつけていく
[P4]	
for character forming	
is embellished with integrity and wisdom	節度と叡智で満たされている
never tarnish	
material possessions	物質的な豊かさ
be flexible and open-minded	
without prejudice, subjectivity or self-righteousness	
[P5]	
this core part of self	自身の核となるこの部分

58

seek convincing answers

vicissitudes of life

[P6]

one's inner spiritual part (spirituality) — 自分の内なる心の部分（スピリチュアリティ）

practical wisdom — 実践的叡智

subconsciously or unconsciously

put the highest priority and value on — ... に最優先の価値を置く

what is my *raison d'être*? — いったい私の存在意義とは何なのか？

modify and reconstruct it

with critical eyes

be easily swayed and sink — 容易に流され、沈んでしまう

try to avoid social pressures in vain — 社会的な圧力から虚しく逃げようとする

[P7]

act as *good aphorisms* for — 良き座右の銘（アフォリズム）となっていく

heartfelt considerations and sincere desires are inscribed in

<Total: 29 Useful Expressions>

6 —Responsive Writing: In Pursuit of Wider Views and Deeper Thoughts—

From the passage, what point(s) have you gained or learned as good hints for making yourself a *prudent and insightful* person? This *Eureka* (new finding) will become a *good medium* for generating a big question or obtaining new knowledge and findings through discussion with your classmates. Describe your *Eureka* in 100-120 words.

My *Eureka* (New Finding) from the Passage   (   ) words

7 —Note Taking and Exchanging Ideas—Listening Practice and Follow-Up Discussion—

Write down keywords, phrases, or important points from your classmates' presentations on *My Eureka*. Then hold a discussion using this information. Try to raise a big question or obtain further new knowledge through active interaction.

8 —Reflection with a Pure Mind—
素心深考　＊Unit 7 からの学び

　Commencement には「始まり」という意味があります。その一方で「（大学での）学位授与式」、つまり卒業式の意味が辞書にあります。始まり―それは人生のほんとうの始まりをさします。「大学卒業＝ほんとうの人生の旅立ち」。この等式が米国大学で伝統的に受け継がれています。"卒業生たちに問う―大学卒業とは単位の修得や成績の優劣を意味するものではない。ならば、ほんとうの意味での卒業の証しとは、いったい何なのか？"これに向けた確認儀式が commencement です。新たな船出、ほんとうの人生の始まり。しっかりオールを握り、漕ぎ出していけるよう、重厚な Aphorism がスピーチに刻み込まれています。

Unit **8**

Justice in the University
With the Right Direction of Politics in Mind

1 —Precept—

In contrast to other animals and species, human beings are blessed with the faculty of language. However, if a person uses language only for showing pleasure or making complaints, it seems immature and childish. This applies to a foreign language as well.

他の動物や種族と違い、人類は言語を操る能力が付与されている。しかし一人の人間が単に自分の喜びや不満を表すためだけに言葉を用いるのであれば、それは未熟で子供じみているように思える。これは外国語にも言えることだ。

2 —Prudence and Insight—

@EpicTop10.com by flickr

　ハーバードを含め、米国の大学で政治学の議論をすることは一つの文化となっているようです。それは大学生たちが市民として政治（国政や地方政治）に積極的に参加していく自覚と責務を感じているからです。<u>それではハーバードの場合、「何を尺度にしながら」正しい政治の姿とその方向性を学生たちに教えようとしているのか、その点について話し合ってください。</u>そこでの「ことばの役割」についても話し合ってください。

ヒント（キーワード）：政治学の目的、正義の捉え方、美徳に対する理解、共通善

Study Focus: Professor Michael Sandel's Idea of Justice in Human Society.

Gist of Each Paragraph

Introduction

[P1] Professor Michael Sandel's brief profile and his world-famous book *Justice – What's the Right Thing to Do*. This book poses a critical question in the argument of *Human Justice* and *Social Justice*, and addresses the purpose of using language in this context.

Body

[P2] Dr. Sandel's ideas about Greed—its definition, its influence, and its concrete emergence in a society centered on economy.

[P3] His ideas about Virtue—its definition, its importance in a good society. His big question: How can or should people judge about virtue?

[P4] He mentions historic political philosophers (e.g., Immanuel Kant, John Rawls) and their ideas of justice and virtue as a good source for critical thinking.

[P5] He introduces Aristotle's idea of what people morally deserve, while calling for the arguments about justice. This is extremely important when focusing on the rights and wrongs of economic impacts and following results in human society.

[P6] His argument—it is time to incorporate *moral reflection* in encountering new situations and in reviewing existing principles in order for exercising *sound judgment*.

[P7] His argument—politics must serve to help people develop their own distinctive human capacities and sense of virtue, especially in order to deliberate about the common good, to acquire practical judgment, to share in self-government, and to care for the fate of the community.

Conclusion

[P8] The connection between human capabilities and language. A crucial role of language is not just for expressing superficial pleasure or pain (surface level). In the realm of politics, it must also serve to help people discern and deliberate about the essence of goodness with a prudent mind.

4 —Main Passage and Oral Reading—

[P1]   Professor Michael Sandel teaches political philosophy at Harvard University. His writings—covering justice, ethics, democracy, markets—have been translated into 27 languages. In 2009, Dr. Sandel published a book titled *Justice – What's the Right Thing to Do*[1]. This publication is useful in assisting today's college students struggle with authentic themes, such as politics, ethics, virtue—all associated with public philosophy. In this book, the role of the faculty of language is also mentioned as crucial. Let's read and consider Dr. Sandel's statements below.

[P2]   Greed is a vice, a bad way of being, especially when it makes people oblivious to the suffering of others. More than a personal vice, it is at odds with civic virtue. In times of trouble, a good society pulls together. Rather than press for maximum advantage, people look out for one another. A society in which people exploit their neighbors for financial gain in times of crisis is not a good society. Excessive greed is therefore a vice that a good society should discourage if it can. Price gouging laws cannot banish greed, but they can at least restrain its most brazen expression, and signal society's disapproval of it. By punishing greedy behavior rather than rewarding it, society affirms the civic virtue of shared sacrifice for the common good.

[P3]   The virtue argument ... rests on a judgment that greed is a vice that the state should discourage. But who is to judge what is virtue and what is vice? Don't citizens of pluralist societies disagree about such things? And isn't it dangerous to impose judgments about virtue through law? In the face of these worries, many people hold that government should be neutral on matters of virtue and vice; it should not try to cultivate good attitudes or discourage bad ones.

[P4]   Modern political philosophers—from **Immanuel Kant**[2] in the eighteenth century to **John Rawls**[3] in the twentieth century—argue that the principles of justice that define our rights should not rest on any particular conception of virtue, or of the best way to live. Instead, a just society respects each person's freedom to choose his or her own conception of the good life.

[P5]   These days, most of our arguments about justice are about how to distribute the fruits of prosperity, or the burdens of hard times, and how to define the basic rights of citizens. In these domains, considerations of welfare and freedom predominate. But arguments about the rights and wrongs of economic arrangements often lead us back to **Aristotle's⁴** questions of what people morally deserve, and why.

[P6]   As we encounter new situations, we move back and forth between our judgments and our principles, revising each in light of the other. This turning of mind, from the world of action to the realm of reasons and back again, is what moral reflection consists in.

[P7]   The purpose of politics is nothing less than to enable people to develop their distinctive human capacities and virtues—to deliberate about the common good, to acquire practical judgment, to share in self-government, to care for the fate of the community as a whole.

[P8]   Nature makes nothing in vain, and human beings, unlike other animals, are furnished with the faculty of language. Other animals can make sounds, and sounds can indicate pleasure and pain. But language, a distinctly human capacity, isn't just for registering pleasure and pain. It's about declaring what is just and what is unjust, and distinguishing right from wrong. We don't grasp these things silently, and then put words to them; language is the medium through which we discern and deliberate about the good. ... So we only fulfill our nature when we exercise our faculty of language, which requires in turn that we deliberate with others about right and wrong, good and evil, justice and injustice.

[628 words]

語 注

Justice – What's the Right Thing to Do¹ 『正義について—なにが正しい行為といえるのか』
Immanuel Kant² イマヌエル・カント。プロイセン（今のドイツ）に生きた哲学者で、ケーニヒスベルク大学の哲学教授を務め、有名な著書に『 純粋理性批判 』、『 実践理性批判 』、『 判断力批判 』などがある。
John Rawls³ 正式名はジョン・ボードリー・ロールズ。アメリカ人の哲学者でハーバード大学教授。有名な著書に『正義論』がある。
Aristotle's⁴ アリストテレス（Aristotle）は古代ギリシャの哲学者でプラトンの弟子にあたる。ソクラテスと弟子のプラトン、そしてプラトンの弟子のアリストテレスの３名は偉大なる哲学者として崇められ、彼らの善なる人間と社会の幸福を考究した姿勢は西洋世界に多大な影響を与えている。

■ Checking Your Oral Reading Speed *Words Per Minute (WPM)*
{Self / Pair / Group}

Measure your WPM using your cellphone or other timing device. Read the passage aloud and determine whether your speed is *sufficient* for reading texts by using the WPM index below.

Words Per Minute (WPM) Index

Total Words ÷ Your Reading Time (in seconds) × 60 = Your WPM
◆   Target WPM = 110 – 125. vs. * *My WPM* = (   )

If your WPM is in the range of the Target WPM, your reading-aloud speed is sufficient to read texts. If your WPM is beyond 125, it is nearing native WPM. If your WPM is below 100, you need to work on your reading speed.

5 —Vocabulary Building—
Important Words / Phrases / Sentences

This vocabulary list contains important words, phrases and sentences from the passage. Using an English-Japanese dictionary or website, please write the Japanese meaning in blank parts.

English	Japanese
[P1]	
struggle with authentic themes	正統的なテーマに取り組む
public philosophy	公共哲学
the role of the faculty of language	ことばがもつ力（言語能力）の役割
as crucial	
[P2]	
it makes people oblivious to the suffering of others	それは人々に他者の苦しみを忘却させようとする
at odds with civic virtue	
in times of trouble, a good society pulls together	困難な時ほど、良い社会は一つになる

press for maximum advantage	最大限の利益を貪る
exploit their neighbors for financial gain	自分の隣人を食い物にしてカネ儲けに奔走していく
price gouging laws	便乗値上げ禁止法
restrain its most brazen expression	あからさまな行動に走ることは抑制できる
signal society's disapproval of it	それを支持しない社会の姿を示す
punishing greedy behavior rather than rewarding it	
shared sacrifice for the common good	共通善のために犠牲を分かち合う

[P3]

the virtue argument ... rests on a judgment	美徳をめぐる議論をみると、... という判断（扱い）に頼っているところがある
citizens of pluralist societies	多元的な共存社会を支持する市民
government should be neutral on matters of virtue and vice	

[P4]

the principles of justice	正義の原則
a just society respects each person's freedom	

[P5]

considerations of welfare and freedom predominate	幸福と自由に対する考察が主流となる
the rights and wrongs of economic arrangements	経済的な取り決めが正しいか間違っているか

[P6]

move back and forth between	
revising each in light of the other	両者に目を向けながら修正していく
this turning of mind ... is what moral reflection consists in	こうした心の変化（折り返し）... によって道徳への考察が成立していく

[P7]

nothing less than to

deliberate about the common good　　共通善について深く考える

share in self-government　　　　　　自己管理に対する共通認識

[P8]

human beings ... are furnished with the faculty　人間 に は... 言語 能力 が 備
　　of language　　　　　　　　　　　　　　　わっている

just for registering pleasure and pain　　快楽や苦痛を表現するためだ
　　　　　　　　　　　　　　　　　　　　けにある

we discern and deliberate about the good

<Total: 30 Useful Expressions>

6 —Responsive Writing: In Pursuit of Wider Views and Deeper Thoughts—

From the passage, what point(s) have you gained or learned as good hints for making yourself a *prudent and insightful* person? This *Eureka* (new finding) will become a *good medium* for generating a big question or obtaining new knowledge and findings through discussion with your classmates. Describe your *Eureka* in 100-120 words.

My *Eureka* (New Finding) from the Passage 　　　　　　 (　　　) words

_____

_____

_____

_____

_____

_____

_____

_____

_____

_____

_____

7 —Note Taking and Exchanging Ideas—Listening Practice and Follow-Up Discussion—

Write down keywords, phrases, or important points from your classmates' presentations on *My Eureka*. Then hold a discussion using this information. Try to raise a big question or obtain further new knowledge through active interaction.

8 —Reflection with a Pure Mind—
素心深考 ＊Unit 8 からの学び

　「正義」とはなにか…。壮大な問いかけゆえ、その定義がまず必要となります。正義の意味を理解し、そのうえで日常生活に応用していく。実践に移していく。それには私利私欲をこえ、社会全体の幸せに通じる「共通善（The Common Good）」に目を向けていく必要があります。そこには市民的美徳と政治的美徳が宿っていなければなりません。こうしたテーマと大学生たちは向き合っていく必要があります。世界で名だたるカリスマ的政治哲学者、マイケル・サンデル教授はハーバードというアゴラ（集会場所）に立ち、世界中から集まった若者たちに正義と政治の深い関係性を訴え続けています。

Unit 9

A Critical Consideration of Today's Market-Oriented Society
Economic Supremacy vs. Morality, Virtue, the Common Good

1 —Precept—

Remember this—politics can be easily overheated when it lacks or belittles morals, ethics, and integrity. Such a shameful politics fails to answer big questions concerning true happiness and human virtue.

　覚えておくがいい。政治とは、そこに道徳、倫理、節度がなく、あるいはないがしろにされている時には、いとも簡単に目的を見失った形で過熱していくものである、ということを。そうした恥ずべき政治は、真の幸福と人間の美徳を巻き込んだ壮大な質問には答えることができない。

2 —Prudence and Insight—

@Pictures of Money by Flickr

　世界共通の主要テーマの１つが政治と経済の関係性です。両者は不即不離、表裏一体の関係にあるとも言えます。経済（モノやカネの豊かさ）を優先して政治をおこなっても、それは正しい政（まつりごと）になる、という等式は成り立ちません。国家としての「真の幸せ」を考えた時、目指すべき「国のかたちとその姿勢（国柄と国是）」はどうあるべきか...。「個（エゴ、自己利益）」よりも「公（共通善）」を大切にし、その成熟した姿を明らかにしていく政治のあり方は重要と言えます。<u>では、正しい政治にはどのような考えが重要になってくるのか、それについて話し合ってください</u>。

ヒント（キーワード）：市場原理中心社会、幸福の意味と実現方法、古代ギリシアの

3 —Understanding the Gist of Each Paragraph of the Main Passage—

Study Focus: Professor Michael Sandel's Skeptical Views on Market-Oriented Human Society.

<u>Gist of Each Paragraph</u>

Introduction

[P1] Professor Michael Sandel's grave concern: the ongoing overheated economy, especially driven by the wave of *market triumphalism*. To him, this social trend fundamentally endangers the issue of Justice in human society (see Unit 8), as well as the issue of human virtue.

Body

[P2] Dr. Sandel's argument—today's politics are more and more controlled by the market and the market economy, and politics are easily overheated due to the lack of moral and spiritual aspects.

[P3] His argument—the main defect of a market-oriented society is that it ignores moral and spiritual aspects such as altruism, generosity, solidarity, and civic spirit.

[P4] His idea and definition of "Moral Excellence" and "Happiness". Plus, the importance of these two agendas in association with Aristotle's idea of what "Moral Virtue" means.

[P5] His explanation about "Becoming Virtuous" (becoming a person of virtue in human society)—using an example of how to play the flute and become dexterous in playing it. In short, what is important is to make it *a habit*. This applies to Aristotle's precept of how to understand and exercise *Practical Wisdom*.

Conclusion

[P6] His statement focusing on Aristotle's Practical Wisdom, including its meaning and role, in association the importance of moral virtue when grappling with today's overheated market economy and market society (*market triumphalism*).

[P1] Dr. Michael Sandel, a Harvard professor, warns of an ongoing overheated social movement caused by the global economy, which has been heavily driven by the wave of *market triumphalism*. In Dr. Sandel's eyes, this trend has unquestionably run the risk of damaging and depreciating the common good in human society. In other words, it has endangered the realm of *public philosophy*. With respect to this emergent issue, he published a book titled ***The Moral Limits of Markets***[1] in 2012 after publishing ***Justice – What's the Right Thing to Do***[2] in 2009. Including the importance of *practical wisdom*, the following messages from Dr. Sandel are beneficial in considering the right direction of politics and human society.

[P2] Our politics is overheated because it is mostly vacant, empty of moral and spiritual content. It fails to engage with big questions that people care about. The moral vacancy of contemporary politics has a number of sources. One is the attempt to banish notions of good life from public discourse. In hopes of avoiding sectarian strife, we often insist that citizens leave their moral and spiritual convictions behind when they enter the public square.

[P3] Altruism, generosity, solidarity, and civic spirit are not like commodities that are depleted with use. They are more like muscles that develop and grow stronger with exercise. One of the defects of a market-driven society is that it lets these virtues languish. To renew public life we need to exercise them more strenuously.

[P4] Moral excellence does not consist in aggregating pleasures and pains but in aligning them, so that we delight in noble things and take pain in base ones. Happiness is not a state of mind but a way of being, "an activity of the soul in accordance with virtue". But why is it necessary to live in a polis to live a virtuous life? Why can't we learn sound moral principles at home, or in a philosophy class, or by reading a book about ethics—and then apply them as needed? **Aristotle**[3] says we don't become virtuous that way. "Moral virtue comes about as a result of habit". It's the kind of thing we learn by doing. "The virtues we get by first exercising them, as also happens in the case of the arts well".

[P5] In this respect, becoming virtuous is like learning to play the flute. No one learns how to play a musical instrument by reading a book or listening to a lecture. You have to practice. And it helps to listen to accomplished musicians, and hear how they play. You can't become a violinist without finding. So it is with moral virtue: "we become just by doing just acts, temperate by doing temperate acts, brave by doing brave acts". ... New situations always arise, and we need to know which habit is appropriate under the circumstances. Moral virtue therefore requires judgment, a kind of knowledge Aristotle calls "practical wisdom".

[P6] Unlike scientific knowledge, which concerns "things that are universal and necessary", practical wisdom is about how to act. It must "recognize the particulars; for it is practical, and practice is concerned with particulars". Aristotle defines practical wisdom as "a reasoned and true state of capacity to act with regard to the human good". ... Practical wisdom is a moral virtue with political implications. People with practical wisdom can deliberate well about what is good, not only for themselves but for their fellow citizens and for human beings in general. Deliberation is not philosophizing, because it attends to what is changeable and particular. It is oriented to action in the here and how. But it is more than calculation. It seeks to identify the highest human good attainable under the circumstances.

[612 words]

語 注

The Moral Limits of Markets[1] 『市場原理主義の道徳的限界をめぐって』
Justice – What's the Right Thing to Do[2] 『正義について—なにが正しい行為といえるのか』
Aristotle[3] アリストテレス (Aristotle) は古代ギリシャの哲学者 (Unit 8 参照)。知的探求を淵源とする哲学の学問的な体系化に成功した結果、それは哲学、倫理、修辞学などの人文学だけでなく、自然科学、芸術の分野までを扱っている。この学術的な偉業から「万学の祖」と呼ばれている。倫理や道徳、美徳、叡智について深く探求した結果、それを『ニコマコス倫理学』に著した。

■ Checking Your Oral Reading Speed *Words Per Minute (WPM)*
{**Self / Pair / Group**}

Measure your WPM using your cellphone or other timing device. Read the passage aloud and determine whether your speed is *sufficient* for reading texts by using the WPM index below.

Words Per Minute (WPM) Index

Total Words ÷ Your Reading Time (in seconds) × 60 = Your WPM

◆ Target WPM = 110 – 125. vs. * *My WPM* = (   )

If your WPM is in the range of the Target WPM, your reading-aloud speed is sufficient to read texts. If your WPM is beyond 125, it is nearing native WPM. If your WPM is below 100, you need to work on your reading speed.

5 —Vocabulary Building—
Important Words / Phrases / Sentences

This vocabulary list contains important words, phrases and sentences from the passage. Using an English-Japanese dictionary or website, please write the Japanese meaning in blank parts.

English	Japanese
[P1]	
an ongoing overheated social movement	今も続く過熱した社会の動き
the wave of *market triumphalism*	市場原理勝利主義のうねり
run the risk of damaging and depreciating the common good	
it has endangered the realm of *public philosophy*	
practical wisdom (* Unit 7)	実践的叡智
[P2]	
empty of moral and spiritual content	
banish notions of good life from public discourse	公共世界から善き生という概念を追い出す

75

in hopes of avoiding sectarian strife　（政治の）党派的な争いを避けたいがために

citizens leave their moral and spiritual convictions behind　国民は道徳的で内面的に確かなものを後回しにする

[P3]

altruism, generosity, solidarity, and civic spirit

the defects of a market-driven society　市場原理主義社会の欠点

it lets these virtues languish　こうした美徳を衰弱させる

[P4]

in aggregating pleasures and pains　快楽と苦痛の差し引き勘定の計算

delight in noble things and take pain in base ones　崇高なものに歓びを感じ、下劣なものに苦痛を感じる

live in a polis to live a virtuous life　有徳な生活を送るために都市国家に住む

sound moral principles　健全な道徳原理

in a philosophy class

moral virtue

[P5]

accomplished musicians　熟練した音楽家

temperate by doing temperate acts　節度ある行動によって節度を身につける

[P6]

recognize the particulars; for it is practical, and practice is concerned with particulars　特定（個別）の状況を認識すること。というのも、それ（実践的叡智）は行動であり、行動は特定の状況と関わっているからだ

with regard to the human good

a moral virtue with political implications　政治的な意味合いを持つ美徳

their fellow citizens　同じ市民

it is oriented to action in the here and how　それはまさにこの場においてどう動くかに向けられている

identify the highest human good

人間として最も気高い善を見極めていく

<Total: 26 Useful Expressions>

6 —Responsive Writing: In Pursuit of Wider Views and Deeper Thoughts—

From the passage, what point(s) have you gained or learned as good hints for making yourself a *prudent and insightful* person? This *Eureka* (new finding) will become a *good medium* for generating a big question or obtaining new knowledge and findings through discussion with your classmates. Describe your *Eureka* in 100-120 words.

My *Eureka* (New Finding) from the Passage   **(   ) words**

_____

_____

_____

_____

_____

_____

_____

_____

_____

_____

_____

7 —Note Taking and Exchanging Ideas—Listening Practice and Follow-Up Discussion—

Write down keywords, phrases, or important points from your classmates' presentations on *My Eureka*. Then hold a discussion using this information. Try to raise a big question or obtain further new knowledge through active interaction.

8 —Reflection with a Pure Mind—
素心深考　＊Unit 9 からの学び

　グローバリズムの拡大と並行しながら市場主義社会（市場原理中心社会）が勢いを増しています。その一方で「実践的叡智とはなにか」という壮大な問いかけに世間の関心が集まっているとは言えません。マモニズム（拝金主義）＋物質的な豊かさ（金欲と物欲）に目がいき、モラル、節度、良識が軽視され、風化されていく恐ろしさ。そうした人間の心の「さもしさ」。それが世界全体に広がりを見せているとするなら、そこには歪んだ経済感覚と悪しき経済政策が跳梁し、善き政治がおこなわれていない可能性があります。サンデル教授は経済（学）と政治（学）の不即不離の関係に目を向けながら節度、冷静、深慮といった心的（内面的）成熟の必要性を訴え続けています。

Unit **10**

Aristotle and *Ethica Nicomachea*
Anatomy of Practical Wisdom

1 —Precept—

If human happiness is brought about by excellent virtue, we need to identify the nature of virtue. Virtue relates to the activity of soul, and only a high quality of soul can give birth to good civic virtue.

　もし人類の幸福は、すぐれた美徳によってもたらされるものであるなら、美徳の本質について、まず明らかにしてみる必要がある。美徳は魂の活動とつながっている。そして高次の魂だけが、すぐれた社会的美徳を生み出してくれる。

2 —Prudence and Insight—

　よりよき社会や人類の幸福といったテーマ（公共哲学）に目を向けた時、欧米の大学はその淵源（古代ギリシャ哲学）にまで遡って考えます。とりわけ今日の学問体系を確立した「学問の祖」として有名な、アリストテレスの考えに目を向けます。ソクラテスの教えは弟子のプラトンに、プラトンの考えは弟子のアリストテレスに受け継がれ、その結果、善き社会と人類の幸福という壮大なテーマは、今日まで議論され続けています。そこでアリストテレスの倫理観とその実践とはどのようなものか、その特徴について話し合ってください。

ヒント（キーワード）：実践的叡智が求められる状況、ニコマコス倫理学、共同社会、幸福と美徳と中庸

Study Focus: Aristotle's Ideas on how to understand and demonstrate wisdom—toward a better human society.

Gist of Each Paragraph

Introduction

[P1] Aristotle's brief profile based on his distinguished feasts—establishment of well-organized education systems and well-categorized academic disciplines (setting up today's study fields in school), and voluminous production of scholarly writings.

[P2] Another of Aristotle's achievements—his thorough study of ethics. His theory: Ethics is a habit (concrete action in daily life), not a subject (knowledge from textbook). Also, virtue cannot be separated from thinking and doing ethics. In the study of ethics, some important aspects are feeling, capacity, and a stable disposition.

Body

[P3] Aristotle's famous book: *Ethica Nicomachea (The Nicomachean Ethics)*. Here, he regards "Pursuit of Happiness, Virtues, the Mean, Community Life" as very important in clarifying the meaning of "Highest Good" of a person and a community.

[P4] In Aristotle's ethics, virtues and the golden mean play pivotal parts in the highest good. He focuses on rational thinking (e.g., prudence and deliberation) and non-rational thinking (e.g., temperance, generosity, truthfulness, and bravery), both of which relate to *the high quality of soul*.

[P5] Remember—humans are political and social beings, so they are responsible for joining in, committing to, examining, and improving politics and human society.

[P6] The hallmark of Aristotle's ethics is called *Practical Wisdom*, and in order to make this wisdom a habit, it is important to be wise rather than clever or shrewd.

Conclusion

[P7] Aristotle's hope and desire through his ethical views—the appearance of authentic personal maturity and real happiness in human society. For this aim, altruism plays a key role.

4 —Main Passage and Oral Reading—

[P1]   Aristotle (384–322 BC, in Ancient Greece) was a great philosopher and a polymath. He is famous for having laid the cornerstone of today's educational system and values, which have been continuously implemented and cherished in Western schools and universities. More famous is his contribution to education through his many scholarly writings. They cover most of today's academic disciplines, including rhetoric, psychology, linguistics, economics, politics, and government (i.e., humanities) as well as physics, biology, zoology (i.e., sciences), metaphysics, logic, ethics (i.e., philosophy) and aesthetics, poetry, theatre, music (i.e., arts).

[P2]   Aristotle's writings cover a wide range of academic fields. However, another great achievement of Aristotle is his treatment of the study of ethics not as knowledge but as real practice in daily life. In an effort to exhibit what ethics means, Aristotle taught and persuaded people to take concrete actions (behaviors), urging them to make them a *habit* in the end. He believed people would be able to exemplify ethics by showing their deeds and attitudes in explicit manners. In this sense, he urged people to be conscious of the nature of virtue. Aristotle weighed three aspects as relevant and important—a feeling (pathos), an inborn predisposition or capacity (dunamis), and a stable disposition that has been acquired (hexis). These ideas are elaborated in his book ***Ethica Nicomachea (The Nicomachean Ethics)[1]***.

[P3]   In *The Nicomachean Ethics*, Aristotle put great value on Pursuit of Happiness, Virtues, the Mean, Community Life. He believed these keywords were indispensable for clarifying and authenticating *the highest good* of a person and a community, being convinced that the highest good is the ultimate happiness for humans and societies. He encouraged people to realize this ultimate happiness by being attentive to altruism rather than egocentrism; that is, to consider the *common good* for the sake of the well-being of human society.

[P4]   For the quest of true happiness and highest good, Aristotle deemed *virtues* and *the golden mean* crucial, as both are essentially connected with a fair-minded spirit and behavior, i.e., an altruistic orientation. Aristotle considered two types of virtues—one related to a high quality of thought such as prudence and deliberation (i.e., rational thinking); the other for non-rational thinking such as temperance, generosity, truthfulness, and bravery. All of these virtues are associated with the quality of the *soul*.

[P5]   Humans are social and political beings, so it does not make sense to separate human happiness and social well-being from the improvement of politics and community engagement. Aristotle's ethics aligned this idea with *virtue, the mean, community*, then added further important keywords such as *continence, end, friendship, habituation, political science, prudence*.

[P6]   For the nurture of virtue, continence and end are critical aspects; meanwhile, friendship fosters a generous and altruistic mind. Prudence is important in guiding political science in the right direction. Aristotle also put great value in habituation, for this regular conduct plays a central part in demonstrating what he termed *Practical Wisdom*. This wisdom is the proof of a person's *good character*—being considerate, temperate, and wise rather than being clever and shrewd, also being deliberate in judging what is good and right, or evil and bad. In other words, the act of exercising practical wisdom indicates a high-level activity of the *soul*, thus this wisdom needs to be linked with and contribute to the common good for human happiness and social well-being.

[P7]   As exemplified in *Ethica Nicomachea*, Aristotle's philosophy is always geared to what is morally important and socially beneficial. Aristotle tells us the importance of becoming a well-balanced human, who ought to be blessed with well-rounded character, prudence, and self-control. All of these are indispensable in promoting altruism. If we miss these core parts of Aristotle's lessons, it will be difficult to bring about true happiness in contemporary society, or even in future society.

[629 words]

語 注

Ethica Nicomachea (The Nicomachean Ethics)[1] 『ニコマコス倫理学』。アリストテレスの代表的著作の１つで、彼が残した多くの倫理学に関する著述を体系立ててまとめあげた作品。息子のニコマコスが編纂に取り組み、この書名はそこから由来している。

■ Checking Your Oral Reading Speed *Words Per Minute (WPM)*
{Self / Pair / Group}

Measure your WPM using your cellphone or other timing device. Read the passage aloud and determine whether your speed is *sufficient* for reading texts by using the WPM index below.

Words Per Minute (WPM) Index

Total Words ÷ Your Reading Time (in seconds) × 60 = Your WPM

◆   Target WPM = 110 – 125.   vs. * *My WPM* = (   )

If your WPM is in the range of the Target WPM, your reading-aloud speed is sufficient to read texts. If your WPM is beyond 125, it is nearing native WPM. If your WPM is below 100, you need to work on your reading speed.

5 —Vocabulary Building—
Important Words / Phrases / Sentences

This vocabulary list contains important words, phrases and sentences from the passage. Using an English-Japanese dictionary or website, please write the Japanese meaning in blank parts.

English	Japanese
[P1]	
a great philosopher and a polymath	
famous for having laid the cornerstone of today's educational system and values	今日の教育制度と教育価値の礎を築いたことで知れ渡る
have been continuously implemented and cherished in	... で長く重宝され、実践に移されている
many scholarly writings	
academic disciplines	学問分野
[P2]	
in an effort to exhibit what ethics means	倫理とはどのようなものかを説明するにあたり
exemplify ethics	

84

in explicit manners	
be conscious of the nature of virtue	
a feeling (pathos)	感情（パトス）
an inborn predisposition or capacity (dunamis)	生まれもった性質あるいは能力（デュナミス）
a stable disposition that has been acquired (hexis)	身につけている安定した性癖（ヘキシス）
these ideas are elaborated in his book	

[P3]

Pursuit of Happiness, Virtues, the Mean, and Community Life	幸福の追求、美徳、中庸、共同体としての生活
indispensable for clarifying and authenticating	... を明らかにし、本物にしていくために不可欠である
being convinced that	... であると確信した
by being attentive to altruism rather than egocentrism	自己中心主義ではなく、利他主義に注意を払いながら
the *common good* for the sake of the well-being of human society	人間社会の幸福に向けた、共通善への思いについて

[P4]

both are essentially connected with a fair-minded spirit and behavior	両者は公平な心と行動と、本質的に結びついている
an altruistic orientation	利他的な志向
prudence and deliberation	
non-rational thinking	非合理的思考
temperance, generosity, truthfulness, and bravery	

[P5]

Aristotle's ethics aligned this idea with *virtue, the mean, community*	アリストテレスの倫理学は、こうした考えを美徳、中庸、共同体と抱き合わせた

[P6]

the proof of a person's *good character*	

[P7]

as exemplified in	... が示すように
Aristotle's philosophy is always geared to	

a well-balanced human

well-rounded character, prudence, and self-
    control

miss these core parts of Aristotle's lessons   こうしたアリストテレスの教
   えの核心部分を見逃す

<Total: 30 Useful Expressions>

6 —Responsive Writing: In Pursuit of Wider Views and Deeper Thoughts—

From the passage, what point(s) have you gained or learned as good hints for making yourself a *prudent and insightful* person? This *Eureka* (new finding) will become a *good medium* for generating a big question or obtaining new knowledge and findings through discussion with your classmates. Describe your *Eureka* in 100-120 words.

My *Eureka* (New Finding) from the Passage　　　　(　　) words

_____

_____

_____

_____

_____

_____

_____

_____

_____

_____

_____

7 —Note Taking and Exchanging Ideas—Listening Practice and Follow-Up Discussion—

Write down keywords, phrases, or important points from your classmates' presentations on *My Eureka*. Then hold a discussion using this information. Try to raise a big question or obtain further new knowledge through active interaction.

8 —Reflection with a Pure Mind—
素心深考　* Unit 10 からの学び

　「今の世の中はおかしい... 正しい方向に向かってはいない」。そう考えるなら、温故知新、つまり歴史からの教訓に目を向けるべきです。歴史に残る賢人たちは、時代の状況と世の中が進む方向性に危惧を抱いていました。それゆえ語り合い、動き、確かな答えを模索しました。アリストテレスは叡智（ウィズダム）の本質にこだわり、考え続けました。金欲や権力よりもそれを監視し、警鐘を鳴らし、諫めていく「正義の番人」としての Wisdom。節制、良識、美徳を武器とするこの存在の具体的な実践（Practical Wisdom）について説きました。当時も紛争や戦争は絶えず、人々は圧政と支配に苦しんでいました。それだけに「良き人間とより良い社会」への考究と希求は真剣でした。叡智について米国大学生たちが考える以上、われわれも「英語で考え、答えを出していく」必要があるのではないでしょうか。

Unit 11

Teaching and Learning Wisdom in the University Developing Historic Insight and Wise Thinking

1 —Precept—

There is no easy path to learning, understanding, and exercising wisdom. Remember—wisdom is not an independent entity; it is comprised of ethics, virtue, history, and other humanistic traits.

　叡智について学習し、理解し、実践していく近道は存在しない。そこで覚えておくがいい。叡智とは単独に出来上がったものではない。倫理、美徳、歴史、それ以外の人道的な特性が合わさったものであることを。

2 —Prudence and Insight—

　古代ギリシア哲学とそこに関わった賢者の思想と理想。そこに目を向け、重きを置く米国の大学。なぜならそこには人類にとって重要な教えと確かな真実が宿っているからです。歴史上の賢人（アリストテレスなど）が唱えた叡智を理解するためにどのような形で教育と学習が行われているのか、それについて話し合ってください。そこでの外国語（学習）の意義と目的についても話し合ってください。

ヒント（キーワード）：叡智（ウィズダム）の定義とIQとの違い、叡智理解の学習方法と指導上のポイント、叡智と動機づけとの関係、外国語（学習）の役割

3 —Understanding the Gist of Each Paragraph of the Main Passage—

Study Focus: Concrete methods of how to teach and learn wisdom in college classroom.

Gist of Each Paragraph

Introduction

[P1]   Professor Robert J. Sternberg, the world-renowned researcher of educational psychology and human development, and the author of an article about the importance of wisdom education at today's college.

Body

[P2]   Prof. Sternberg's definition of wisdom—the application of intelligence, creativity, knowledge to the common good in human society.

[P3]   His idea of differentiating Intelligent Quotient (IQ) from wisdom.

[P4]   Also the difference between motivation and wisdom.

[P5]   His suggestion of how college students can foster a good sense of wisdom by reading *Great Books* (i.e., classics and modern works).

[P6]   His explanation of how to conduct wisdom education concretely.

Conclusion

[P7]   His argument focusing on why learning a foreign language is important in the study of wisdom.

4 —Main Passage and Oral Reading—

[P1]   Dr. Robert J. Sternberg is a world-renowned researcher of educational psychology and human development, who has taught at Yale University and Cornell University (both Ivy League Universities). In a book titled ***Wisdom in the University***[1] (2007), Professor Sternberg and his colleagues wrote an article titled "Teaching for wisdom: what matters is not just what students know, but how they use it." For the comprehensive study of what *Wisdom* means and why it exists, concrete ideas and suggestions are presented in this article. Interestingly, the purpose of foreign language learning is also stressed.

90

[P2] Wisdom is defined as the application of intelligence, creativity, and knowledge as mediated by values toward the achievement of a common good. Thus, wisdom is not just about maximizing one's own or someone else's self-interest, but also about balancing off self-interests with the interests of others and of other aspects of the context in which one lives.

[P3] Dr. Sternberg accounted for the fundamental difference between IQ and wisdom as follows:

Increases in intelligence—at least as measured by IQ—have not been matched by obvious comparable increases in wisdom. Indeed, to the extent that our society has increasingly stressed the use of IQ to maximize one's own chances of admission to and success in the 'cognitive elite' ... increases in IQ may have been concomitant with decreases in wisdom. High IQ with a scarcity of wisdom has brought us a world with the power to finish itself off many times over. Wisdom might bring us a world that would seek instead to better itself and the conditions of all the people in it.

Wisdom is not only connected with IQ, but also with other aspects such as motivation, learning strategies and teaching approaches, as well as goals for learning and using a foreign language.

[P4] If one's motivations are to maximize certain people's interests and minimize other people's, wisdom is not involved. In wisdom, one seeks a common good, realizing that this common good may be better for some than for others.

[P5] Students will develop wisdom by becoming engaged in class discussions, projects, and essays that encourage them to discuss the lessons they have learned from both classical and modern works, and how these lessons can be applied to their own lives and the lives of others. They can study not only the truths, but also the values.

[P6] Students often want large quantities of information spoon-fed or even force-fed to them. They then attempt to memorize this material for exams, only to forget it soon thereafter. In a wisdom-based approach to teaching, however, students will need to take a more active role in constructing their learning by:

(1) Reading classic works of literature and philosophy (whether Western or otherwise) to learn and reflect on the wisdom of the

sages.

(2) Engaging in class discussions, projects, and essays that encourage them to discuss the lessons they have learned from the literary and philosophical works they've read, and how these lessons can be applied to their own lives and the lives of others.

(3) Studying not only about 'truth' but also 'value (sense of value)' through reflective thinking.

(4) Exercising critical, creative, and practical thinking in the service of good ends and the common good.

[P7] The foreign language classroom is another terrain for enhancing students' wise thinking skills. Foreign languages should be taught in the cultural context in which they are embedded, requiring students to engage in reflective and dialogical thinking to grasp the foreign culture and to position themselves and their experiences in relation to this culture. ... There is no easy road to wisdom. ... How we use it will determine the fate of our society and of others.

[607 words]

語 注

Wisdom in the University[1] 『大学で取り組む叡智についての学び』

■ Checking Your Oral Reading Speed *Words Per Minute (WPM)*
{Self / Pair / Group}

Measure your WPM using your cellphone or other timing device. Read the passage aloud and determine whether your speed is *sufficient* for reading texts by using the WPM index below.

Words Per Minute (WPM) Index

Total Words ÷ Your Reading Time (in seconds) × 60 = Your WPM

◆ Target WPM = 110 – 125. vs. * *My WPM* = (   )

If your WPM is in the range of the Target WPM, your reading-aloud speed is sufficient to read texts. If your WPM is beyond 125, it is nearing native WPM. If your WPM is below 100, you need to work on your reading speed.

5 —Vocabulary Building—
Important Words / Phrases / Sentences

This vocabulary list contains important words, phrases and sentences from the passage. Using an English-Japanese dictionary or website, please write the Japanese meaning in blank parts.

English	Japanese
[P1]	
educational psychology and human development	教育心理と人間発達（学）
the purpose of foreign language learning is also stressed	外国語学習の目的も重視されている
[P2]	
as mediated by values toward the achievement of a common good	共通善の実現を目指していく価値観を媒介にした
maximizing one's own or someone else's self-interest	自分や他者の個人的な利益を最大化していく

English	Japanese
balancing off self-interests with the interests of others and of other aspects of	自己利益と他者利益、そして ... での他の観点もみながらバランスを保っていく

[P3]

English	Japanese
chances of admission to and success in the 'cognitive elite'	「知的エリート」の入学とその成功の機会
concomitant with decreases in wisdom	叡智の衰退が同時に発生する
high IQ with a scarcity of wisdom	
a world with the power to finish itself off many times over	その力で何度もこの世界を終わりにしてしまう

[P4]

English	Japanese
maximize certain people's interests and minimize other people's	特定集団の利益を最大化し、それ以外の人たちの利益を最小化していく

[P5]

English	Japanese
by becoming engaged in class discussions, projects, and essays	... を議論し、プロジェクトを立ち上げ、エッセイ（小論文）にまとめてみることで
both classical and modern works	
not only the truths, but also the values	

[P6]

English	Japanese
want large quantities of information spoon-fed or even force-fed	大量の情報を口元まで運んでくれたり、強制的に与えてくれることを望んでいる
take a more active role in	
classic works of literature and philosophy	文学と哲学の古典的な作品
how these lessons can be applied to their own lives	学んだ教訓と、それが自身の生活にどう生かしていけるのか
through reflective thinking	
the service of good ends and the common good	善き目的と共通善に向けて

[P7]

English	Japanese
another terrain for enhancing students' wise thinking skills	賢明な思考を高めていくさらなる領域

the cultural context in which they are embedded

それが関与する文化的状況

position themselves and their experiences in
relation to this culture

この文化（外国文化）に関連
づけて自身とわが体験を照
らし合わせていく

<Total: 22 Useful Expressions>

6 —Responsive Writing: In Pursuit of Wider Views and Deeper Thoughts—

From the passage, what point(s) have you gained or learned as good hints for making yourself a *prudent and insightful* person? This *Eureka* (new finding) will become a *good medium* for generating a big question or obtaining new knowledge and findings through discussion with your classmates. Describe your *Eureka* in 100-120 words.

My *Eureka* (New Finding) from the Passage   (   ) **words**

_____

_____

_____

_____

_____

_____

_____

_____

_____

_____

_____

7 **—Note Taking and Exchanging Ideas—Listening Practice and Follow-Up Discussion—**

Write down keywords, phrases, or important points from your classmates' presentations on *My Eureka*. Then hold a discussion using this information. Try to raise a big question or obtain further new knowledge through active interaction.

8 **—Reflection with a Pure Mind—**
素心深考　* Unit 11 からの学び

　ウィズダム（叡智）の教育と学習について、アイビーリーグのイェール大学とコーネル大学での教歴をもつ著名な心理学者（教育心理学者）ロバート・スタンバーグ教授のアプローチに注目が集まっています。Wisdom—この本質とその実践をどのように学生たちに教え、学ばせ、理解を促し、自分のことばで表現させ、定義させていくことができるのか…。そこに目を向けた授業づくりをされています。注目すべきはそこでの外国語（学習）の意義と役割です。叡智を知り、実践していくうえでの外国語学習とは…。一流の大学教授の「目のつけどころ」は、やはり違います。

Unit 12

The Dawn of Japan's Commitment to Western Values (1)
Fukuzawa Yukichi and *Bunmeiron no Gairyaku*

1 —Precept—

If civilization is defined as the yardstick of living standards and social outlook, and these two are gauged solely by material affluence and technological advancement, this concept completely ignores the original meaning and the spirit of civilization in the U.S. and Europe.

　文明とは、物質的な豊かさと技術的な進歩によって推し量られる生活水準と社会の姿であるとするなら、この見方は米国やヨーロッパが抱く本来の意味と精神をまったく無視していることになる。

2 —Prudence and Insight—

　福澤諭吉は自身の渡米と渡欧体験（国際感覚の獲得と錬磨）をもとに「文明論の概略」を世に出しました。武士社会と封建制度から解放された明治期に入り、欧米を軸にした西洋列強への仲間入りに日本が奔走していた頃、福澤は海外経験と膨大な原書精読を通して欧米社会がもつ「文明の正しき姿」を考究し続けました。その結果、文明とは表面的で物理的な姿とその進展をさすものではなく、精神性（スピリチュアリティ）を巻き込んだ、じつに深いものである、と悟りました。では、欧米人からみた文明の姿（civilization）とはどのようなものか、福澤が出した答えについて考えてみてください。そこには日本人特有の国民性や精神性に対する戒めが含意されています。

ヒント（キーワード）：知識、道徳、個人世界と公共世界、高い次元での人間的生活

3 —Understanding the Gist of Each Paragraph of the Main Passage—

Study Focus: The challenge of Japan's internal (spiritual) Westernization (1): Fukuzawa Yukichi's views on true civilization.

Gist of Each Paragraph

Introduction

[P1]   Fukuzawa Yukichi's brief profile and his conviction of what civilization means in the context of Western values (virtue, good character, wisdom).

[P2]   His argument focus—civilization should be evaluated not on external matters but on internal ones.

Body

[P3]   His explanations—some crucial components that comprise authentic civilization.

[P4]   His warning—do not look at material aspects alone; rather, think about human refinement first.

[P5]   His precept—look at both material (outer) and spiritual (inner) aspects then try to keep them in good balance. In the latter, never ignore or trivialize virtue.

[P6]   Also, in order for self-growth and self-enlightenment, try to keep a good balance between the expansion of knowledge and the empowerment of virtue.

Conclusion

[P7]   The goal of Keio Gijuku (his school)—training students to be true civilized people, and the ideal character of a Keio Graduate (as a proof of a matured person).

4 —Main Passage and Oral Reading—

[P1]   Fukuzawa Yukichi is a well-known person in Japanese history. While establishing Keio Gijuku (his school), Fukuzawa advocated and introduced Western values and spirit into Japan at the end of Edo era, i.e., prior to the Meiji era of Japan's westernization and internationalization.

Struggling to establish modern Japan, he published articles and books, and they were helpful in bringing Japanese citizens' way of thinking and views closer to the U.S.-European standards. Especially, *Bunmeiron no Gairyaku* (文明論之概略 *An Outline of a Theory of Civilization* in 1875) elaborately depicts Fukuzawa's prudent thoughts and keen observations on Western civilization; namely, the emphasis of virtue, good character, and wisdom for good society. Let's consider the following statements written in this book.

[P2] The civilization of a country should not be evaluated in terms of its external forms. Schools, industry, army and navy, are merely external forms of civilization. It is not difficult to create these forms, which can all be purchased with money. But there is additionally *a spiritual component*, which cannot be seen or heard, bought or sold, lent or borrowed. Yet *its influence on the nation is very great*.

[P3] We must first know what we mean by civilization. It is extremely difficult to describe in concrete terms, and, at one extreme, there are even some who dispute whether civilization is good or bad. Now, when we inquire into the reasons for such a dispute, we find that "civilization" can be understood in both a broad and a narrow sense. In the narrow sense "civilization" merely means the increase of what man consumes and of the superficial trappings added on to daily necessities. In its broad sense "civilization" means not only comfort in daily necessities but also the refining of knowledge and the cultivation of virtue so as to elevate human life to a higher plane.

[P4] What, then, does civilization mean? I say that it refers to the attainment of *both* material well-being *and* the elevation of the human spirit. It means both abundance of daily necessities and esteem for human refinement. Is it civilization if only the former is fulfilled? The goal of life does not lie in food and clothes alone. If that were man's goal, he would be no different from an ant or a bee. This cannot be what Heaven has intended for man.

[P5] Therefore, there must be both material and spiritual aspects before one call it civilization. Moreover, there is no limit to the material well-being or the spiritual refinement of man. By material well-being and spiritual refinement is meant a state in which these two aspects are really making progress, and by civilization is meant the progress of both man's well-being and his refinement. Since what produces man's well-being and refinement is knowledge and virtue, civilization ultimately means the progress of man's knowledge and virtue. ... Ignorance and lack of virtue are diseases of civilization.

[P6]   Since intelligence and morality split man's heart, as it were, into two, and each controls its own proper sphere, there is no way of saying which is the more important. Both are needed to make a complete human being. ... Now, knowledge and virtue, together, are as necessary for civilized society as the presence of both vegetables and grains and fish and meat is to a healthy diet for the human body.

[P7]   In Keio Gijuku, until graduation, we concentrate on training the students to acquire good judgment. When the training is completed and the students graduate, we let them go their own ways, and we do not interfere in their behavior. We hope our true alumni will be outspoken when they express themselves, but when they stay silent, truly silent. We do not take interest in this random world where the advocates are ignorant, the listeners, too are ignorant, and the unlearned and unreasonable masses are heading toward no clear goal.

[644 words]

■   Checking Your Oral Reading Speed   *Words Per Minute (WPM)*
{Self / Pair / Group}

Measure your WPM using your cellphone or other timing device. Read the passage aloud and determine whether your speed is *sufficient* for reading texts by using the WPM index below.

Words Per Minute (WPM) Index

Total Words ÷ Your Reading Time (in seconds) × 60 = Your WPM
◆   Target WPM = 110 – 125. vs. * *My WPM* = (   )

If your WPM is in the range of the Target WPM, your reading-aloud speed is sufficient to read texts. If your WPM is beyond 125, it is nearing native WPM. If your WPM is below 100, you need to work on your reading speed.

5 —Vocabulary Building—
Important Words / Phrases / Sentences

This vocabulary list contains important words, phrases and sentences from the passage. Using an English-Japanese dictionary or website, please write the Japanese meaning in blank parts.

English	Japanese
[P1]	
advocated and introduced Western values and spirit into Japan	西洋の価値観と精神を称揚し、日本に紹介した
establish modern Japan	
Japanese citizens' way of thinking and views	
elaborately depicts	... を精細に描く
prudent thoughts and keen observations on Western civilization	西洋文明についての深い考えと鋭い観察
[P2]	
should not be evaluated in terms of its external forms	
a spiritual component	内面的なもの（心の部分）
[P3]	
we must first know what we mean by civilization	
even some who dispute whether civilization is good or bad	その良し悪しをめぐる議論さえも
"civilization" can be understood in both a broad and a narrow sense	「文明」とは広義にも狭義にも捉えることができよう
the increase of what man consumes and of the superficial trappings	消費物（モノ）の増加であり、... に貼り付けられた罠（巧みな誘い文句）の増大
the refining of knowledge and the cultivation of virtue	
elevate human life to a higher plane	人としての生活をより高次に導く

[P4]

    it refers to the attainment of *both* material well-being *and* the elevation of the human spirit | それは物質的な安寧と人間精神の高揚（成熟）の両方の確立をさす

[P5]

    both material and spiritual aspects

    by material well-being and spiritual refinement is meant a state | 物質的安寧と心の洗練とは ... の状態をさす

    the progress of both man's well-being and his refinement

    the progress of man's knowledge and virtue

    ignorance and lack of virtue are disease of civilization

[P6]

    intelligence and morality split man's heart | 知性と道徳が心に存在し

[P7]

    we do not interfere in their behavior | 我々は彼（女）らの行動に干渉しない

    our true alumni | 真の卒業生

    We do not take interest in this random world where the advocates are ignorant, the listeners, too are ignorant, and the unlearned and unreasonable masses are heading toward no clear goal | 声高に言う人間が無知であり、聴衆も無知であり、無学で理性をもたない大衆が、明確な目標をもたずに進んでいく荒唐無稽な世に関心をもつことなく ...

<Total: 23 Useful Expressions>

6 —Responsive Writing: In Pursuit of Wider Views and Deeper Thoughts—

From the passage, what point(s) have you gained or learned as good hints for making yourself a *prudent and insightful* person? This *Eureka* (new finding) will become a *good medium* for generating a big question or obtaining new knowledge and findings through discussion with your classmates. Describe your *Eureka* in 100-120 words.

My *Eureka* (New Finding) from the Passage   (   ) **words**

_____

_____

_____

_____

_____

_____

_____

_____

_____

_____

_____

7 —Note Taking and Exchanging Ideas—Listening Practice and Follow-Up Discussion—

Write down keywords, phrases, or important points from your classmates' presentations on *My Eureka*. Then hold a discussion using this information. Try to raise a big question or obtain further new knowledge through active interaction.

8 —Reflection with a Pure Mind—
素心深考 ＊Unit 12 からの学び

　苦労して磨きをかけたオランダ語。この外国語に精通していた一介の下級武士が、日本の歴史的大転換をもたらす開国に目をつけ、鋭く先手を打ったのが「英語時代＆西欧化時代の到来とその教育」でした。咸臨丸で渡米し、米国の人々、事物、生活に衝撃を受け、その後の渡欧によるさらなる視野の拡大....。英語を介して欧米世界を正しく理解し、その本質を理解することに福澤諭吉は磨きをかけました。その努力の結晶が『文明論の概略』として著されました。いわく、西欧を知ることとは、異彩を放つ人々（知識人、良識人など）の人格をまず知り、わが身に当て嵌め、わが心に焼き付け、わが内面世界を充実させることにある、と。それによって真の人間としての独立と自尊が可能となる...。そこに行きついたのです。

Unit 13

The Dawn of Japan's Commitment to Western Values (2)
Nitobe Inazo and *Touzai Ai Furete*

1 —Precept—

What is the next stage of civilization? Whatever it may be, it should not be characterized solely by further progress of science and technology. When talking about civilization, we should never forget to focus on humanism and altruism instead of materialism and mammonism.

　文明の次なる姿とはどういうものか？一つ警告しておきたいことは、それは科学と技術のさらなる発展だけで証明されるものではない、ということだ。文明を口にする時、物質主義や拝金主義ではなく、人道主義と利他主義を巻き込んでいくことを忘れるべきでない。

2 —Prudence and Insight—

　新渡戸稲造は「武士道」を英語で著わし、それは *Bushido* として世界的名著になりました。福澤と同じく日本の夜明け（国際化）に尽力し、その卓越した英語力と豊かな国際感覚、そして世界平和への希求は国際連盟の事務次長という要職に就いたことからわかります。この天職に人生を捧げた結果、一つの集大成として名著「東西相触れて」が出版されました。福澤諭吉と同じく「正しき文明の姿」を追い求めた新渡戸は、成熟した人間社会と世界全体の姿について明確な答えを出しています。それはどのようなものか、話し合ってください。

ヒント（キーワード）：武士道の意味、世界共通となる善と悪の捉え方、昔の偉人が残した幸福への貴重な教え、人間社会の正しい姿

—Understanding the Gist of Each Paragraph of the Main Passage—

Study Focus: The challenge of Japan's internal (spiritual) Westernization (2): Nitobe Inazo's emphasis on sophisticated human nature with a proper sense of morality.

Gist of Each Paragraph

Introduction

[P1]   Nitobe Inazo's brief profile and theory of how to understand the Western world (based on his book titled *Tozai Ai Furete*), as well as the Japanese traditional spirit (his book titled *Bushido*).

Body

[P2]   His big question—"What is the next form of civilization?" (with an image of an ideal human society).

[P3]   His explanation of what Bushido means.

[P4]   His image of the purpose of human society—based on core spiritual values of Bushido.

[P5]   His argument—moral rather than material progress must be more important in considering what citizenship means and what citizens ought to be.

[P6]   His warning—introducing Thomas Carlyle's precept, that is, the aiming to decrease desire because it grows to be infinite. According to him, humans need to be modest and have integrity to avoid being greedy.

Conclusion

[P7]   Drawing on Shakespeare's *King John*—begging for money and richness should never become the golden standard in human life.

4 —Main Passage and Oral Reading—

[P1]   When **the League of Nations**[1] was established in 1920, Nitobe Inazo became one of **the Under-Secretaries General of the League**[2]. Dr. Nitobe is internationally famous for his English-written book ***Bushido: The Soul of Japan***[3] (1900). He however wrote another famous book ***The Japanese Nation: Its Land, Its People, and Its Life − With Special***

Consideration to Its Relations with the United States[4] (1912). Admittedly, the essence of this book is based on his Japanese book titled *Tozai Ai Furete* (東 西 相 触 れ て). This English-version successfully witnesses the core teachings of Dr. Nitobe, which value human spirituality beyond cultural and regional borders. Here, he also cherishes the precepts left by sages who lived in much older times. Let's listen to his statements with these points in mind, considering his deep understanding of what Western civilization is.

[P2]   One of the most interesting and serious questions that confront the world today is—Whither are we bound? Or, to put is another word—*What is to be the next form of civilization?* ...man's general progress lies in his growing more universal in knowledge and in sympathy, in broadening his education so as to embrace the East and the West.

[P3]   Bushido, which furnished the nation at large with the canons of right conduct, was originally, as I have explained, intended only for the samurai, and the tradespeople were little thought of in its scheme, or perhaps more accurately, the tradespeople little thought of it. The common, every-day, democratic virtues of honest dealing, prudence, cheerfulness, diligence, were held secondary to the highest virtues of patriotism, loyalty, friendship, benevolence, and rectitude.

[P4]   Broad views of humanity, the recognition of a world-standard of right and wrong, the deepening of personal responsibility—irrespective of race or nation—are too often sadly lacking in the systems of ethics and in the religions proposed.

[P5]   We will at least give credit to our forefathers, however, for their noble idea; for, after all, ideas are seeds—as long as they do not lose their vitality. The absence of moral factors in our educational system is a matter of serious concern. In our haste to construct the nation on a new basis, the political and material institutions of the West were largely adopted, because we believed, rightly or wrongly, that it was in these that the West excels us. But in course of time, it became evident that without emphasizing the moral side of life, material progress was fraught with more danger than is adherence to old traditions. We are not merely subjects, but citizens, not only citizens of Japan but of the world-community.

[P6]   Our old masters taught us to increase the quotient not by increasing the numerator, or the supply of things, but by decreasing the denominator, our desires. Infinity can be procured, as **Thomas Carlyle**[5] taught, by reducing our covetousness. Modern civilization, however, does not tolerate old-time simplicity. Bread! Bread!!—sour or sweet—leavened or unleavened—bread has become the first and last cry in this modern age.

[P7]   As wrote **Shakespeare in *King John*[6]**: "Well, whiles I am a beggar, I will rail, And say—there is no sin, but to be rich; And being rich, my virtue then shall be, To say—there is no vice but begging." The logic of this sad cynicism leads to the universal adoption of a "gold standard" for all concerns of life. As at the devil's booth, all things come to be sold or bartered for bread. Poverty, despicable in our industrial age, as it was in the religion of **Mammonism**[7], is the gravest of sins. Gauged by the physical standard, Japan certainly stands low among the nations.

[600 words]

語 注

the League of Nations[1]　国際連盟（現在の国際連合の前身的な役割をもつ国際機関）

the Under-Secretaries General of the League[2]　国際連盟事務次長（事務総長の補佐役）

Bushido: The Soul of Japan[3]　『武士道―日本人の品格』

The Japanese Nation: Its Land, Its People, and Its Life – With Special Consideration to Its Relations with the United States[4]　『日本という国―土地、人々、生活―米国との深き絆に思いを込めて』

Thomas Carlyle[5]　19世紀に活躍した英国人歴史家で、批評家でもある。スコットランド出身。代表作として『衣装哲学』、『英雄崇拝論』などがある。「世界の歴史は英雄によって作られる」と述べたことで有名だが、ここでいう「英雄」とは人類史上に影響を与えた神や預言者、詩人、僧侶、文人、詩人など、幅広い意味で用いられている。

Shakespeare in *King John*[6]　世界的に有名なイギリスの劇作家、ウィリアム・シェイクスピアが手掛けた歴史劇「ジョン王／King John」のこと。正式な題名は『ジョン王の生と死』（The Life and Death of King John）。

Mammonism[7]　マンモニズム―拝金主義のこと。マモン（Mammon）とは新約聖書に出てくる「富」を意味する言葉だったが、それはやがてキリスト教文化圏において「物質的な富」あるいは「貪欲」を意味するようになった。

■ Checking Your Oral Reading Speed **_Words Per Minute (WPM)_**
{Self / Pair / Group}

　Measure your WPM using your cellphone or other timing device. Read the passage aloud and determine whether your speed is *sufficient* for reading texts by using the WPM index below.

Words Per Minute (WPM) Index

Total Words ÷ Your Reading Time (in seconds) × 60 = Your WPM

◆　Target WPM = 110 – 125.　vs.　* *My WPM* = (　　　　)

　If your WPM is in the range of the Target WPM, your reading-aloud speed is sufficient to read texts. If your WPM is beyond 125, it is nearing native WPM. If your WPM is below 100, you need to work on your reading speed.

5 —Vocabulary Building—
Important Words / Phrases / Sentences

　This vocabulary list contains important words, phrases and sentences from the passage. Using an English-Japanese dictionary or website, please write the Japanese meaning in blank parts.

English	**Japanese**
[P1]	
successfully witnesses the core teachings of	... の教えの真髄が見事に示されている
admittedly	
cherishes the precepts left by sages who lived in much older times	遠い昔に生きた賢人たちの遺訓を大切にしている
[P2]	
Whither are we bound?	我々（人類）がどこへ向かっているのか
[P3]	
Bushido, which furnished the nation at large with the canons of right conduct	武士道は国としての正しき振る舞いを示した教典

the tradespeople were little thought of in its scheme	商人はその範疇になく
democratic virtues of honest dealing, prudence, cheerfulness, diligence	深慮、陽気さ、勤勉さを扱う誠実な市井人としての美徳
were held secondary to	... の後にまわされていた
the highest virtues of patriotism, loyalty, friendship, benevolence, and rectitude	

[P4]

irrespective of race or nation	
in the systems of ethics and in the religions proposed	倫理綱領と声高に唱えられている宗教をみる限り

[P5]

give credit to	... を褒め称える
a matter of serious concern	深刻な懸念事項
our haste to construct the nation on a new basis	日本は新しい土台の上に国造りを急いだ
in course of time	
fraught with more danger	
adherence to old traditions	

[P6]

our old masters	先哲（過去に生きた賢人たち）
increase the quotient not by increasing the numerator ... but by decreasing the denominator	モノの供給（分子）を増やすのではなく、欲望（分母）を減らすことで全体の値は増していく
infinity can be procured	無限性を手に入れることができる
modern civilization, however, does not tolerate old-time simplicity	今日の文明は昔日の質素に対して寛容ではない
bread! bread!!	パンだ！パンをよこせ！（もっとモノが欲しい！）

[P7]

whiles I am a beggar, I will rail	オレが乞食である間は、自分を罵倒するだけよ

there is no vice but begging	乞食ほどの悪はない
the universal adoption of a "gold standard" for all concerns of life	人生（生き方）すべてに対する不文律（金科玉条）の広範な受け入れ
at the devil's booth	悪魔がする屋台
gauged by the physical standard	

\<Total: 27 Useful Expressions\>

6 —Responsive Writing: In Pursuit of Wider Views and Deeper Thoughts—

From the passage, what point(s) have you gained or learned as good hints for making yourself a *prudent and insightful* person? This *Eureka* (new finding) will become a *good medium* for generating a big question or obtaining new knowledge and findings through discussion with your classmates. Describe your *Eureka* in 100-120 words.

My *Eureka* (New Finding) from the Passage   **(   ) words**

7 —Note Taking and Exchanging Ideas—Listening Practice and Follow-Up Discussion—

Write down keywords, phrases, or important points from your classmates' presentations on *My Eureka*. Then hold a discussion using this information. Try to raise a big question or obtain further new knowledge through active interaction.

8 —Reflection with a Pure Mind—
素心深考 ＊Unit 13 からの学び

　新渡戸稲造は福澤の文明観に共感していました。すなわち外見ではなく、内面部分（スピリチュアリティ）の重要性に新渡戸も気づいていました。この部分の成熟なくして人間としての成功、人生の成功、そして世界の幸福は実現できないと信じていました。米国ジョンズホプキンス大学（全米最古の大学院大学）で博士号を取得し、米国人女性と結婚。そして国際連盟の事務次長として世界の幸福と安寧に向けて尽力しました。モノ、カネ、権力ではなく、もつべきは美徳、思いやり、良心、節度...。ここに人間としてのモラルがあり、そこには国籍、人種、宗教宗派の壁は関係してこない。新渡戸は名著『東西相触れて』を通して、この真実を説きました。

Unit 14

The Dawn of Japan's Commitment to Western Values (3)
Joseph Hardy Neesima and Doshisha English School

1 —Precept—

What is good character? I know it because I learned it through college-based American educational style and Christianity. If asked about good character is, I will say this word first of all, that is, "Conscience".

　良い人格とはなにか？それについて、私は知っている。アメリカでの大学教育とキリスト教を通して学んだのだから。良き人格について問われたなら、真っ先に私はこう答えるだろう。それは「良心（の持ち主）だ」と。

2 —Prudence and Insight—

@663highland

　福澤諭吉や新渡戸稲造と同じく、新島襄は身につけた英語力と国際感覚を武器に明治の黎明期に活躍し、西洋人の成熟した精神尺度（価値観、崇高な心、冷静な判断基準）から日本人と日本国のあるべき姿と進むべき道について考究し、答えを出しました。同志社設立を通して新島が訴えたその答えとはどのようなものか、そして英語（教育）についてどのような目的を抱いていたか、話し合ってください。

ヒント（キーワード）：英語（外国語）を学ぶ目的、英語力の使い道、キリスト教主義の教育と日本の理想の姿、同志社が目指す人間像

115

3 —Understanding the Gist of Each Paragraph of the Main Passage—

Study Focus: The challenge of Japan's internal (spiritual) Westernization (3): Joseph Hardy Neesima's ideas and desire for English-mediated character education in Japan.

Gist of Each Paragraph

Introduction

[P1]   Joseph Hardy Neesima's brief profile and his motive for establishing Doshisha (his school) in Japan.

Body

[P2]   His vision—the aim of founding Doshisha Academy (originally Doshisha English school).

[P3]   His belief—manifesting Christianity as the central pillar of Doshisha education, with an emphasis on moral education.

[P4]   His passion—Doshisha must educate individuals to be well-equipped with knowledge, integrity, and wisdom.

[P5]   His most important value—acquiring and demonstrating conscience as the hallmark of Doshisha education. This is the most important part of human refinement.

[P6]   His desire—each student's real independence, that is, thinking, judging, and acting on his/her own with strong mentality and morality.

Conclusion

[P7]   The global person must be flexible and open-minded in accepting different values and cultures. Exercising a good command of English (and other foreign languages) must be crucial as part of understanding what is going on around the world.

4 —Main Passage and Oral Reading—

[P1]   Niijima Jō (新島 襄), née Niijima Shimeta (新島 七五三太), a.k.a. Joseph Hardy Neesima in the United States, is a Japanese missionary and educator of the Meiji era who established Doshisha English School (later

Doshisha University). In 1864, when national isolation was still in effect and people were forbidden to go abroad, Niijima broke the law and secretly smuggled into the United States. In his new life there, Joseph Hardy Neesima attended **Phillips Academy**[1] from 1865 to 1867 and then graduated from **Amherst College**[2] in Massachusetts. Neesima became the first Japanese to obtain a bachelor's degree in the United States. After his return, he established his English language school based on Christian values, imbuing his all thoughts, ideas, desires, and precepts in Doshisha. The following statements from the Doshisha University website successfully express the *Neesima Spirit*.

[P2]   *The purpose of founding Doshisha Academy was not only to equip students with a general knowledge of the English language, but also to cultivate ... virtue, enhance their integrity, and help them discipline their mind. In other words, we have made every effort to produce individuals who are able to put their conscience into practice. Such education can never be achieved only through intellectual education.*

[P3]   *We placed Christianity at the core of the fundamentals of moral education, believing our ideal education can be achieved only by Christian moral teachings, which include devout faith, pursuit of truth and compassion for others.*

[P4]   *It is not the power of a few heroes that maintains a nation. Education, knowledge, wisdom, and integrity are central to those who build and run society. We, at Doshisha, aim to produce individuals with such characteristics. It is ingrained in our ethos that our ultimate purpose lies in nurturing the people, who shall be called 'the conscience of the nation'.*

[P5]   *'Conscience' is the principle that underpins Doshisha's educational philosophy. Our founder, Joseph Neesima, through his nine years spent in Western countries, realized that Christianity, especially* **Protestantism**[3]*, significantly influenced the Western culture and mind. For Neesima, an important aspect of Christianity was that conscience grows not before the eyes of humans but before the eyes of God. He believed that one can become a true human being by cultivating conscience, and that conscience can be effectively inspired through an education based on Christian principles. It appeared to Neesima that education in Japan emphasized intellectual development more than the cultivation of the mind.*

[P6]   *By instilling conscience in students, as well as providing academic knowledge and professional skills and building a strong mentality and morality, the founder of Doshisha, Joseph Neesima, aimed to nurture individuals who can think independently without being influenced by external forces and create change on their own initiative through the guidance of their conscience. Nurturing students' ability to act independently and helping them to realize their full potential, Doshisha has long respected the independent and unconventional mind. We trust students' growing capabilities, respect their individuality, and encourage them to act on their own initiative by fully exercising their abilities.*

[P7]   Doshisha aims to develop *individuals who are not only competent in foreign languages, but can also accept the different values of other cultures and discover something meaningful from them. On awakening to the importance of education after visiting America and studying there, Neesima decided to establish an institution of higher learning, Doshisha University, in his homeland. We, as a successor to his aspirations, have placed emphasis on fostering a global outlook and perspective in learning. We provide students with the opportunity not only to learn a foreign language as a communication tool, but also to become immersed in a different culture, understand the similarities as well as the differences of other cultures compared to our own, and learn to respect these diversities.*

[624 words]

語 注

Phillips Academy[1]　米国マサチューセッツ州にある歴史ある有名私立校。独立戦争中の 1778 年に男子校として設立され、1973 年に隣接する名門女子校アボット・アカデミー（1829 年設立）と合併し、現在は男女共学校になっている。

Amherst College[2]　マサチューセッツ州アマーストにある私立のリベラルアーツ校。学士課程教育を重視し、人格形成を重んじている。人文学と自然科学などを包摂した教養科目群（自由学芸：リベラルアーツ）を大切にし、知性、感性、そして人格の円満な形成を目指している。新島襄の卒業をもとに Amherst College は同志社大学と姉妹関係を確立し、深い学術交流を続けている。

Protestantism[3]　プロテスタント（英：Protestant）は宗教改革運動によってカトリック教会（または西方教会）と袂を分かち、福音主義を理念とするキリスト教を展開する諸教派による教義をさす。日本の場合、カトリック教会（旧教）に対し、「新教」（しんきょう）と呼ばれている。

■ Checking Your Oral Reading Speed *Words Per Minute (WPM)*
{Self / Pair / Group}

Measure your WPM using your cellphone or other timing device. Read the passage aloud and determine whether your speed is *sufficient* for reading texts by using the WPM index below.

Words Per Minute (WPM) Index

Total Words ÷ Your Reading Time (in seconds) × 60 = Your WPM
◆ Target WPM = 110 – 125. vs. * *My WPM* = (   )

If your WPM is in the range of the Target WPM, your reading-aloud speed is sufficient to read texts. If your WPM is beyond 125, it is nearing native WPM. If your WPM is below 100, you need to work on your reading speed.

5 **—Vocabulary Building—**
Important Words / Phrases / Sentences

This vocabulary list contains important words, phrases and sentences from the passage. Using an English-Japanese dictionary or website, please write the Japanese meaning in blank parts.

English	Japanese
[P1]	
national isolation	鎖国政策
secretly smuggled into the United States	米国へ密航した
a bachelor's degree	
English language school based on Christian values	キリスト教主義の英語学校
imbuing his all thoughts, ideas, desires, and precepts in	自らの思い、考え、願い、教訓を... に注ぎ込んだ
[P2]	
Doshisha Academy	同志社英学校
cultivate ... virtue	美徳を養い
enhance their integrity	

119

help them discipline	... を鍛えていくその支援にある
put their conscience into practice	
only through intellectual education	
[P3]	
we placed Christianity at the core of the fundamentals of moral education	キリスト教を道徳教育の中心に置き
devout faith	敬虔な信仰
pursuit of truth	真実の追求
compassion for others	
[P4]	
produce individuals with such characteristics	そうした特性を擁した人材の育成
our ethos that our ultimate purpose lies in nurturing the people	究極目的は...（の）人間を育てることであり、それが本学の精神
[P5]	
conscience	
become a true human being by cultivating conscience	
an education based on Christian principles	
[P6]	
building a strong mentality and morality	強い精神と道徳心を構築する
without being influenced by external forces	外から揺さぶられることなく
on their own initiative through the guidance of their conscience	良心の指導を通して自ら率先して
Doshisha has long respected the independent and unconventional mind	
[P7]	
accept the different values of other cultures	
on awakening to the importance of education	教育の重要性に気づき
establish an institution of higher learning	高等教育機関の設立
as a successor to his aspirations	彼の意志を継ぐ者として

<Total: 28 Useful Expressions>

6 —Responsive Writing: In Pursuit of Wider Views and Deeper Thoughts—

From the passage, what point(s) have you gained or learned as good hints for making yourself a *prudent and insightful* person? This *Eureka* (new finding) will become a *good medium* for generating a big question or obtaining new knowledge and findings through discussion with your classmates. Describe your *Eureka* in 100-120 words.

My *Eureka* (New Finding) from the Passage   (   ) words

_____

_____

_____

_____

_____

_____

_____

_____

_____

_____

_____

_____

7 —Note Taking and Exchanging Ideas—Listening Practice and Follow-Up Discussion—

Write down keywords, phrases, or important points from your classmates' presentations on *My Eureka*. Then hold a discussion using this information. Try to raise a big question or obtain further new knowledge through active interaction.

8 —Reflection with a Pure Mind—
素心深考 ＊Unit 14 からの学び

　新渡戸と同じく新島襄も米国で充実した時間を過ごし、日本人として初めて米国大学を卒業し、学士号を取得しました（マサチューセッツ州、アマーストカレッジにて）。キリスト教徒として「良心（Conscience）」を核にした人間教育の実現を我が天命と悟り、それを母国で実践すべく、同志社を設立しました。そこで "英語を習い、使っていくのは何ゆえか" を明らかに示しくいく教育活動を展開しました。それは語学力をこえた、人間構築力への挑戦でもありました。英語（外国語）によってわが心を清め、わが心を磨き、わが魂にゆさぶりをかけ、さらなる高みにわが身をつれていく。さいごは格調高き、品性あふれた人間となり、日本のため、世界のために貢献していく。そうした英語人（国際人）を輩出していくことが新島の願いでした。その精神は同志社に受け継がれています。福澤、新渡戸に並び、新島も「欧米人にひけをとらない英語力と人間完成度、そして冴えきった国際感覚を携えた日本人の育成」に尽力し続けました。

Unit 15

What is the English Language for You?
Gazing at Your Success in Life and Character Development

1 —Precept—

One requirement of entering U.K. & U.S. universities is the demonstration of holistic learning strategies, and these capabilities are aimed at successful character formation as well. The goal of foreign language education is in tune with this admission policy. We Japanese acknowledge this as truth, shouldn't we?

英国・米国の大学入学要件として、高い視点をもった学習方略の構築があげられる。そしてこの能力は、確かな人格形成にも向けられている。外国語教育の目的はこの入学要件と軌を一にしている。我々日本人は、一つの真実としてこのことを認識している。そうではないか?

2 —Prudence and Insight—

米国や英国の大学が示したぶれない教育方針(入学試験の目的と内容、卒業式、公共哲学、叡智学習など)。グローバル時代と新たな英語学習の動機づけ。重要な人生儀式である大学卒業式。叡智(ウィズダム)の理解と実践。古(いにしえ)の人々(賢人、哲学者、日本を真の国際化に導いた英語の達人たち)。こうした多くの「考えるヒント」をもとに、大学での英語学習とはいかなるものか—それについて視点を広げ、考えを深めながら答えを模索してきました。このテキストでの学習を締め括りにあたり、「私がもつべき英語」「私を成長させ、成熟させてくれる英語」とはどのようなものか、答えを出してみてください。あなた自身のにんげんとしての「たしなみ」が、そこに示されているはずです。

ヒント（キーワード）：「自己成熟＝英語成熟」の等式証明に向けた自身の考え、信念、価値観、人生目標

3 —Understanding the Gist of Each Paragraph of the Main Passage—

Study Focus: Overall reflections on what you have leaned and recognized from this textbook.

Gist of Each Paragraph

Introduction

[P1]   Your hopes and expectations for encountering a new style of English education at college/university—different from *Juken*-style English or high school English.

[P2]   One big question: If your memories of learning and using English are *negative*, what is the main cause? Think about it.

Body

[P3]   Reminder—College admission tests in Japan rarely emphasize the aspects of self, identity, character of the examinees.

[P4]   Reminder—Generally, these tests put little weight on (or fundamentally ignore) the applicants' social views, world views, philosophy of life.

[P5]   Review—In the U.S. and the U.K., especially in top-notch universities, the applicants' foremost duty is to explain "Who I really am" comprehensively. That is, they must demonstrate academic intelligence, skills of logic, rhetoric, analysis, lateral thinking and critical thinking, and human beliefs, values, and character.

[P6]   These world-renowned schools have a common admission policy—Assessing the maturity of inner spirit of prospective students. This is very important for both college enrollment and college graduation.

Conclusion

[P7]   Two big questions for you. "What is a university for?" & "What is the English language for?" Generating your own answers to these questions is crucial for the sake of your successful college life and successful engagement with English.

4 —Main Passage and Oral Reading—

[P1] As a college student, sitting in the classroom and taking English classes, you must be excited to encounter a *new mode* of English language education. You hope the style avoids emphasizing memorization of words and idioms, along with frequent quizzes on grammar and usage. You also desire to avoid English-Japanese translation (*Wayaku*) and repetitive rote and pattern-based practices guided by the instructor.

[P2] If your memories of high school English are traumatic, bitter, and demotivating, what do you think is the *main cause*? Besides seeking high scores in written tests, listening tests and mock exams, could you find a *GOOD* reason or goal for learning English? As you can see, this question directly relates to whether or not you could secure a chance to think seriously about the meaning of a foreign language, as well as to understand the ontology of the English language with respect to your successful self-growth (rather than language skills) as a top priority. Did you ever have a chance to use English to describe your own self, such as "who I am, what I want to be, and what I ought to be as a person living in this world?"

[P3] College admission tests in Japan, including the *Daigaku Nyugaku Kyotsu Test* (the major nationwide standardized test for college admission), rarely prepare questions focused on *the self* and *identity*. The tests rarely ask college applicants to exemplify their ideas of what good character formation means. However, you must keep in mind that these areas are essential for the study of good human society, considering public philosophy at college.

[P4] Also, in terms of college admission policy, entrance examinations in this country traditionally put less emphasis on the issues of social views, world views, and philosophy of life. Such examinations rarely ask about the extent to which the applicant is aware of what is going on in local and global societies. The lack of such admission policies and selection strategies may seem *odd* when compared to those of Western colleges and universities.

[P5] In the United Kingdom and the United States, whether through interviews or personal written statements, the applicant's foremost duty is to describe *who I really am as a person*. For both native language and foreign language applicants, the English speaking-and-writing test is utilized to assess the degree of successful character formation, which is equivalent to a high level of academic knowledge and a sophisticated scholarly mind. This engagement is the *traditional value* of college admissions in the two countries, especially in world-renowned top-notch schools like Oxbridge and the Ivy League.

[P6] Again, the crucial requirement of entering U.K. & U.S. universities lies in the development of *holistic* learning strategy and good character. This is the minimum requirement in preparation for joining real world after graduation. A *Matured Person* ought to be achieved during the undergraduate period. It indicates your abilities to face and handle authentic topics and issues using English (and of course Japanese), ranging from ethics, morality, virtue, wisdom, the common good, to success in life—all *moving and spiritually awakening themes* in the U.S. and the U.K., and in other Western countries. All of these regions value Ancient Greek Philosophy as the root of good analytical thinking, good logic, and good rhetoric for the quest of right answers.

[P7] "What is college for?" and "What are my goals for entering and graduating from university?" As a college student, you must answer these questions. You must also prepare your answer for "What is the English language? How does it relate to my life, my future, and human society?" as a practitioner of English. You final duty is to answer this question: "What kind of society will be best for us humans, not just for us who live now, but also for our future generations?" Answering these questions constitutes the sign of your maturity and the proof of your matured way of using English.

[647 words]

■ Checking Your Oral Reading Speed *Words Per Minute (WPM)*
{Self / Pair / Group}

Measure your WPM using your cellphone or other timing device. Read the passage aloud and determine whether your speed is *sufficient* for reading texts by using the WPM index below.

Words Per Minute (WPM) Index

Total Words ÷ Your Reading Time (in seconds) × 60 = Your WPM
◆ Target WPM = 110 – 125. vs. * *My WPM* = (　　　)

If your WPM is in the range of the Target WPM, your reading-aloud speed is sufficient to read texts. If your WPM is beyond 125, it is nearing native WPM. If your WPM is below 100, you need to work on your reading speed.

5 —Vocabulary Building—
Important Words / Phrases / Sentences

This vocabulary list contains important words, phrases and sentences from the passage. Using an English-Japanese dictionary or website, please write the Japanese meaning in blank parts.

English	Japanese
[P1]	
encounter a *new mode* of English language education	
frequent quizzes on grammar and usage	
repetitive rote and pattern-based practices	単調でパターン化した活動
[P2]	
directly relates to whether or not you could secure a chance to	（と）直結しているのは、...の機会があったかどうか、という点だ
the ontology of the English language	英語の存在論（存在意義）
with respect to your successful self-growth (rather than language skills) as a top priority	確かな自己成長（言語スキルではなく）を最優先することについて

[P3]

college admission tests in Japan

rarely prepare questions focused on *the self* and | 自己性とアイデンティティに
 identity | 焦点を当てた質問はまず用
 | 意されていない

exemplify their ideas of | 自分たちの考えを具体化する

you must keep in mind that | ... に留意すべきだ

these areas are essential for | こういった領域は ... で重要
 | になる

[P4]

put less emphasis on the issues of | ... の問題をあまり重視して
 | いない

the extent to which the applicant is aware of

[P5]

a sophisticated scholarly mind | 洗練された学究心

world-renowned top-notch schools

[P6]

the crucial requirement of | ... に向けた大事な要件

holistic learning strategy and good character | 大局観に立った学習方略

ranging from ethics, morality, virtue, wisdom, | 倫理、道徳、美徳、叡智、共
 the common good, to success in life | 通善から人生の成功まで

all *moving and spiritually awakening themes* | 心をくすぐり、精神を溌剌と
 | させるテーマ

Ancient Greek Philosophy as the root of good | 優れた分析的思考、優れた論
 analytical thinking, good logic, and good | 理、優れた説得技法のお手
 rhetoric | 本として、古代ギリシャ哲
 | 学を大事に扱っている

for the quest of right answers

[P7]

as a practitioner of English | 英語を操る人間として

constitutes the sign of your maturity | 自身の成熟の証しとなる

the proof of your matured way of using English

<Total: 24 Useful Expressions>

6 —Responsive Writing: In Pursuit of Wider Views and Deeper Thoughts—

From the passage, what point(s) have you gained or learned as good hints for making yourself a *prudent and insightful* person? This *Eureka* (new finding) will become a *good medium* for generating a big question or obtaining new knowledge and findings through discussion with your classmates. Describe your *Eureka* in 100-120 words.

My *Eureka* (New Finding) from the Passage   (   ) **words**

_____

_____

_____

_____

_____

_____

_____

_____

_____

_____

_____

7 **—Note Taking and Exchanging Ideas—Listening Practice and Follow-Up Discussion—**

Write down keywords, phrases, or important points from your classmates' presentations on *My Eureka*. Then hold a discussion using this information. Try to raise a big question or obtain further new knowledge through active interaction.

8 **—Reflection with a Pure Mind—**
素心深考　* Unit 15 からの学び

　Unit 1 から振り返ると、英語について、大学について、そこでの学びについて、人間社会について、内面性（スピリチュアリティ）と人格について、叡智についてなど、多くの視点（学習テーマ）から「*Soul Searching Trip*（魂の拠りどころを求める旅)」を進めてもらいました。米国と英国の大学入試が求めている価値観と信念、そして人間的魅力。拡大し続けるグローバル社会だからこそ、冷静なマインドで考えてみるべき英語（学習）の存在意義とモチベーションの育み方...。米国の大学卒業式でのスピーチの意味や「正義」を巻き込んだ政治（学）の捉え方と叡智学習の意義。後世のために獅子奮迅した幕末〜明治期の 3 名の偉人たち＝英語の達人。英語とは何なのか。「自己成熟とは英語成熟なり。その逆も真なり。」―この命題を解いていくことに意味があるのです。

Unit 1 College Entrance Examinations in the United States:
        The Purpose of Written Statements Focusing on "Who I am"

Columbia University
https://undergrad.admissions.columbia.edu/apply/process/columbia-questions

Dartmouth College
https://admissions.dartmouth.edu/glossary-term/essay

Princeton University
https://admission.princeton.edu/apply/princeton-supplement

Unit 2 College Entrance Examinations in the United Kingdom:
        The Aim of Interviews Focusing on "Who I am"

Cambridge University Undergraduate Study
https://www.undergraduate.study.cam.ac.uk/applying/interviews/what-do-interviews-involve

Oxford University Undergraduate Admissions Office
https://www.ox.ac.uk/admissions/undergraduate/applying-to-oxford/guide/interviews

Unit 3 The New Direction of English Learning Motivation:
        Looking into the Core Part of Self

Ushioda, E. (2011). Why autonomy? Insights from motivation theory and research. *Innovation in Language Learning and Teaching, 5*(2), 221–232. doi:10.1080/17501229.2011.577536

Ushioda, E. (2011). Language learning motivation, self and identity: Current theoretical perspectives. *Computer Assisted Language Learning, 24*(3), 199–210. doi:10.1080/09588221.2010.538701

Ushioda, E., & Chen, S. (2011). Researching motivation and possible selves among learners of English: The need to integrate qualitative inquiry. *Anglistik, 22*(1), 43-61.

Unit 4 Teaching and Learning English in the Era of Globalization:
        Ontology of a Foreign Language

Ushioda, E. (1996). *Learner autonomy 5: The role of motivation.* Dublin: Authentic language learning resources.

Ushioda, E. (2006). Language motivation in a reconfigured Europe: Access, identity, autonomy. *Journal of Multilingual and Multicultural Development, 27*(2), 148-161. doi:10.1080/01434630608668545

Ushioda, E. (2011). Language learning motivation, self and identity: Current theoretical perspectives. *Computer Assisted Language Learning, 24*(3), 199–210. doi:10.1080/09588221.2010.538701

Ushioda, E. (2013). Foreign language motivation research in Japan: An ʻinsiderʼ perspective from outside Japan. In M. Apple, D. Silva, & T. Fellner (Eds.), *Language learning motivation in Japan* (pp. 1-14). Bristol, U.K.: Multilingual Matters.

Unit 5   Mission and Purpose of College Education:
          Cherishing Eternal Truths

Colby, A., Ehrlich, T., Beaumont, E., & Stephens, J. (2003). *Educating citizens: Preparing America's Undergraduates for lives of moral and civic responsibility. San Francisco, CA: Jossey-Bass.*

Boyer, E. L. (1987). *College: The undergraduate experience in America.* New York: Harper & Row.

Harvard College
https://college.harvard.edu/about/mission-vision-history

University of Chicago
https://college.uchicago.edu/student-life/introduction-annual-lecture-aims-education

Unit 6   Unchanging Values at the University:
          In Consideration of Good Character and Good Society

Simmons, R. J. (2001). President's address to Brown University Community. *Journal of College and Character, 2*(1), Article 2, 1-4. doi: org/10.2202/1940-1639.1285

Unit 8   Justice in the University:
          With the Right Direction of Politics in Mind

Sandel, M. J. (2009). *Justice: What's the right thing to do?* New York: Farrah, Straus and Giroux.

Unit 9   A Critical Consideration of Today's Market-Oriented Society:
          Economic Supremacy vs. Morality, Virtue, the Common Good

Sandel, M. J. (2009). *Justice: What's the right thing to do?* New York: Farrah, Straus and Giroux.

Sandel, M. J. (2012). *What money can't buy: The moral limits of markets.* New York: Farrah, Straus and Giroux.

Unit 10   Aristotle and *Ethica Nicomachea*:
          Anatomy of Practical Wisdom

Ross, W. D. (1966). *The works of Aristotle (Translated into English under the Editorship of W. D. Ross, M.A.). Volume IX.* (*Ethica Nicomachea* by W. D. Ross; *Magna Moralia* by St. George Stock; *Ethica Eudemia* by J. Solomon). Oxford University Press.

Unit 11   Teaching and Learning Wisdom in the University:
          Developing Historic Insight and Wise Thinking

Sternberg, R., Reznitskaya, A., & Jarvin, L. (2008). Teaching for wisdom: What matter is not just what students know, but how they use it. In R. Barnett & N. Maxwell (Eds.). *Wisdom in the university* (pp. 47-62). New York: Routledge.

Unit 12   The Dawn of Japan's Commitment to Western Values (1):
          Fukuzawa Yukichi and *Bunmeiron no Gairyaku*

Kiyooka, E. (1985). *Fukuzawa Yukichi on Education: Selected Works.* Tokyo: University of Tokyo Press.

Fukuzawa, Y. (2008). *An Outline of a Theory of Civilization* (Revised translation by David A. Dilworth and G. Cameron Hurst, III). Tokyo: Keio University Press.

Unit 13   The Dawn of Japan's Commitment to Western Values (2):
          Nitobe Inazo and *Touzai Ai Furete*

新渡戸稲造 (1970).『新渡戸稲造全集　第 13 巻 (The Japanese Nation: The Intercourse between the United States and Japan)』東京：教文館

新渡戸稲造 (1970).『新渡戸稲造全集　第 14 巻 (JAPAN: Some Phrases of her Problems and Development)』東京：教文館

Unit 14   The Dawn of Japan's Commitment to Western Values (3):
          Joseph Hardy Neesima and Doshisha English School

History and Educational Philosophy, About Doshisha, Doshisha University Website

The Purpose of the Foundation of Doshisha University
https://www.doshisha.ac.jp/en/information/history/policy.html

Founding Spirit and Joseph Neesima
https://www.doshisha.ac.jp/en/information/history/neesima/neesima.html

Conscience Education and Educational Philosophy
https://www.doshisha.ac.jp/en/information/history/educational_ideal.html

テキストの音声は、弊社 HP　https://www.eihosha.co.jp/
の「テキスト音声ダウンロード」のバナーからダウンロードできます。
また、下記 QR コードを読み込み、音声ファイルをダウンロードするか、
ストリーミングページにジャンプして音声を聴くことができます。

In Search of Authenticity of Self and English
良質なテキストで自己成熟 ＆ 英語成熟をめざして

2024 年 1 月 15 日　初　版

著　者　©金　岡　　正　　夫
　　　　©米　岡　　ジ ュ リ

発 行 者　佐　々　木　　　元

発 行 所　株式会社　英　　宝　　社
　　　　　〒 101-0032 東京都千代田区岩本町 2-7-7
　　　　　電話 03-5833-5870　FAX03-5833-5872
　　　　　https://www.eihosha.co.jp/

ISBN 978-4-269-13017-3 C1082
印刷・製本：日本ハイコム株式会社